Until The Last Dog

Until The Last Dog

One Man's Lifelong Journey to Alaska with his Dogs

ROB DOWNEY

Dedication

◆

This book is dedicated to my late sister, Fran, who loved to travel the world but never got on a plane or a cruise ship. She read voraciously about many of the most fascinating places on earth. When we would get together, she was just as excited to hear about my latest adventure as she was to read about the places in her book. She loved my Alaskan stories and hearing about all the other faraway places I would visit on business. Every year, she would say, You must write a book! She was my on-the-phone traveling partner as I made the long drives to and from Alaska, or down south on business. Her husband had passed away a few years before she did in 2020, so while driving by myself I called her to talk, and it always helped me stay awake. She made me promise that I would write this book each of the last times we were together before she passed.

Contents

Foreword

I have known Rob Downey for nearly 40 years as a professional colleague, a dog musher, and most importantly as a friend. Through those years I have developed a deep appreciation for Rob, not just for what he does, which as you read this book you will find is quite impressive, but more for the way he does things. As you turn the pages ahead, the story that unfolds will elicit wonder, tears, and laughter. I know because I lived many of those experiences with Rob. You will find a boy who rose above trauma and found his calling through the healing from this event. Rob has built his career and his life around his passionate relationship with his dogs. You will find moments where his very soul was tested by personal injury and loss. What you won't find is a victim. Every challenge is described with disarming honesty, while you may feel empathy for him, you will never feel pity because each low point is followed by a triumph, each challenge is regarded as a learning experience and through the rollercoaster you are treated to Rob's humor and his humility.

I had the privilege of traveling thousands of miles across North America racing sled dogs with Rob. Although we often competed against each other, it was never a rivalry, but more of a brotherhood. Rob won many races, but his focus was never winning. In racing, his dogs always came first. This drive to do the best he could for his dogs, led Rob to start Annamaet Petfoods, a company he named after his mother. He wanted to make the best possible food for his dogs, not based on cost but on what they needed to reach their potential. A truly novel approach in an ultracompetitive industry. Sticking to this initial vision with integrity has resulted in a global phenomenon benefitting a whole generation of pets and their owners. When you read on, you will find that this story is also the story of a phoenix rising from the ashes, but I'll let Rob fill in the details on that one.

Just as winning was not his focus in dog mushing, profit was never his focus in Annamaet. Rob has used his knowledge and his resources to benefit so many. The late George Attla, Alaska Native and 10 time World Champion dog musher, started a dog mushing program to support healthy lifestyles for young people in his home village. Rob joined his friend George in this dream that eventually spread across 17 villages in interior Alaska. Rob has never sought recognition for this, he gave back to the people, dogs and sport that has given him so much because he had the means and the opportunity to do so. This quiet gesture has had a tremendous impact. This is who Rob is and how he does things.

As you'll soon discover, Rob is an outstanding storyteller. His humble, self-deprecating approach to this craft will have you simultaneously spellbound and splitting your sides with laughter. When you read about his harrowing moose encounter, that was followed by years of moose themed gifts from friends, you'll begin to get a feel for Rob's special ability to use humor as a cornerstone of resilience. This book was not Rob's idea. He was urged to put onto paper, the experiences that not only moved, but transformed those of us who were lucky enough to share them with him. I hope that as you read these pages, you will not only understand, but feel the kindness, empathy, pain, hope, and triumph Rob has shared with you. At a time when we are faced, everywhere we look, with things that divide us, this book shows us, in so many ways, the important things that hold us together. Before there was Ted Lasso and the Greyhounds, there was, in real life, Rob Downey and his dog team. Enjoy the ride!

Arleigh Reynolds, D.V.M., Ph.D., D.A.C.V.I.M. (Nutrition)
Professor Emeritus, Veterinary Clinical Nutrition
Director Emeritus, Center for One Health Research
The University of Alaska Fairbanks

Introduction

◆

Like many people, dogs have been a big part of my life. Unlike many people, they have saved my life twice. I grew up with a love of the outdoors and dogs, and honestly all I have ever wanted to do was work with dogs. They have been a constant in my life, leading to a change in my major in college to become a companion animal nutritionist. Dogs also helped me find my wife Mary Jo, who has been my rock and my partner for this entire journey. We were blessed to have two wonderful children, Sarah and Alex, who grew up living and working with dogs along with us. Our dogs have also helped us build Annamaet Petfoods, a company we started and named after my mom Anna Mae who I no doubt got my love of animals from.

My love of dogs has led to almost 40 years competing in sled dog races from the Patagonia region at the southern tip of South America to the Pyrenees Mountains of Spain. But the most enjoyable part of my career was the 20 years I competed in races in Alaska against the best competition in the world. This also led to me driving our dogs back and forth to Alaska along the famed Alaska highway for all those years, in the dead of winter. Temperatures at our cabin in the interior of Alaska would frequently reach -40 degrees with only three hours of daylight. I have also been fortunate enough to have encountered some of the most majestic wildlife in North America. One of these encounters didn't exactly turn out so well.

Hopefully you will enjoy my story, that of a simple man who has been blessed with many amazing dogs, a wonderful family, and a truly fascinating life.

The Moose Story

◆

An Alaskan moose can be six feet tall at the shoulder and can weigh upwards of 1,400 pounds. They are not easily intimidated, and encounters in the wild can be dangerous, if not fatal. A cow (momma) moose is also very protective of her calves. If you happen to visit one of our great national parks out west, you will often hear park rangers say that the single most dangerous animal you will encounter is not a grizzly bear; it is not a timber wolf; it is a cow moose with a calf. A moose on the trail is one of the biggest concerns for an Alaskan sled dog racer, more commonly known as a *dog musher*. Seeing a moose while out on a training run or during a race is not as rare as one would think. A single moose on the trail is cause for concern, but often, they will get out of the way if you give them their space. Moose confrontations vary from year to year, often because of snow levels. In a heavy snow year, you tend to see more moose on the trail because it is much easier for moose to walk on a groomed and packed sled dog trail than it is to wallow around in chest-deep snow in the surrounding forest.

It's not just the packed snow that makes dog trails attractive to moose in heavy snow. In the fall, before the snow arrives, dog mushers spend a lot of time out on the trails trimming back the willows for a clear trail. It can be very painful to get smacked in the eye by an overhanging willow as you are cruising down the trail at about twenty miles per hour with your dog team. Continually trimming back the willows then creates a thick overgrowth along the sides of the trails. This provides a virtual salad bar for moose to walk along the dog trail eating fresh willows. An adult moose will eat about forty pounds of willows per day in the coldest part of winter—enough to fill a fifty-five-gallon trash can. In the interior of Alaska, the snow often starts to fall in late September and will stay all winter until breakup in late April. Moose remain a potential danger for most of the year.

We spent twenty winters, starting in the early '90s, in the interior of Alaska, training and racing our sled dogs. The first few winters, we stayed with very dear and generous friends during the racing season—with all our dogs. I would drive from our home in Bucks County, Pennsylvania, in December or January with the dogs, typically twenty-four to twenty-eight of them, and drive home in late March. It was a 4,200-mile drive each way.

My first trip to Alaska was in December of 1989. At that time, the winters were typically much colder than they are now, which can influence moose behavior. Winters of very cold temperatures and deep snow mean moose burn more calories, so they have to eat more to maintain body weight. We would have weeks where the temperatures would hover between 35°F and 45°F below zero. This increased hunger can make a moose more agitated and angrier, and thus more confrontational if people encounter them on the trail. Most of my dog musher friends in Alaska carry a gun in case they encounter an angry or charging moose.

An angry cow moose- ears back, hackles up, and smacking her lips
Photo credit: © Cecoffman

Early in the season in Fairbanks, the Alaska Dog Mushers Association hosts a series of one-day preliminary races before the big championship series begins in February and March. These preliminary races are a great opportunity for young dogs to get race experience and to try different combinations of dogs as well. Though most people know about the Iditarod, a thousand-mile race that runs between Anchorage and Nome, there is an older, more established type of sled dog racing that happens worldwide called *sprint racing*. The average speed of the Iditarod is around seven to nine miles per hour and the dog team and musher camp out on the trail during the entire race. A sprint mushing team averages twenty to twenty-three miles per hour, depending on the size of the team and the distance raced. There are classes in sprint racing that range from four-dog teams to unlimited, where you can race as many dogs as you can handle, typically twelve to sixteen dogs. The distances are between four miles for the smaller teams and twenty miles for the big teams. Depending on the race length, races last from twenty minutes to an hour, and the races are typically two- to three-day events. We compete in sprint racing as I prefer going fast, but I also prefer to do my camping in the summer as opposed to sleeping outside in the winter at –20 or –40°F. I think my dogs prefer sleeping in a warm bed as well.

One Sunday evening after a preliminary race, I was feeling pretty good. We had finished first for the third preliminary race in a row, and the dogs looked great. We were ready for the championship season to begin! A few of my dog-mushing neighbors came over to our cabin, and we put a couple of frozen pizzas in the oven and had a couple of beers while we talked about the race that day. Before the night was over, they started giving me a hard time for not carrying a gun for moose protection while training. It's not that I am afraid of guns or haven't handled them—I grew up hunting, so I have handled guns from a young age. Honestly, I just wasn't comfortable thinking about safely shooting at a moose from the back of the sled with my dog team between me and the moose. I joked that I would be like Barney Fife; I would be shaking so much that I would most likely shoot one of my lead dogs by mistake. We all laughed.

The next day, my life would be forever changed by this habit.

The next morning, it was –35°F; and I don't train in temperatures colder than –20°F. I had a team of yearlings that really needed to go out for a training run. It finally warmed up to –20°F at 1:00 p.m., and I thought this might be the only chance I have to get them out for a few days. They were fired up, all excited, and ready to roll. With no reins on a dog team, the only control you have is your voice and a claw brake if that fails. I was running an eight-dog team with seven young males weighing an average of sixty-two pounds—some big, strong boys with a lot of power. The eighth dog was a small older female in the lead named Satin, who was there to provide control. Lead dogs are the key. They are your steering wheel. The connection between the musher and his lead dogs is pretty special. You must trust them to turn right or left on command, and the good ones are so tuned-in to you, that you can even move a little to the right or a little to the left side of the trail, depending on conditions. Based on the size of the team, your leaders could be seventy feet in front of you, so they may see things on a turn or at a sweeping curve that you might not see right away. That day, we were several miles down the trail, and I gave a "gee" command for a right-hand turn (a left turn is a "haw" command). I understand these are old horse training terms. No idea how horse training commands entered the sled dog vernacular, but that is a story for another day.

As my leaders made the right-hand turn off the main trail, they backed off like they saw something. I assumed it was a rabbit or a squirrel. We turned off the main trail to go around a big, long loop back in the bush that would eventually bring us back to the main trail heading in the opposite direction toward home. Just as it is difficult for a tractor-trailer to make a U-turn, it is difficult for a seventy-foot-long dog team to make a U-turn on a trail that might be only six feet wide. That is why we have these turnarounds off the main trail on these out-and-back trails. From the air, the trail would look sort of like a big lollipop turnaround in the bush.

As we got to the back side of the loop, we ran straight into a cow moose with a calf. I quickly realized that this was what the dogs must have seen as they were turning off the trail. I was now facing my worst nightmare! I slammed on the brake as I was worried she was going to come into my dog team and start stomping and kicking my dogs. I had heard many stories of dogs being severely injured or even killed by an angry moose. The moose was standing there within a few feet of my dogs; she was on one side of the trail and her calf on the other. My dogs were no longer full of excitement; they just lay down scared and motionless. She flattened her ears against her head and raised her hackles. I could tell she was pissed. I thought it would only be a matter of seconds before she would be in the middle of my dog team, kicking and stomping. I tried to distract her by making myself big on the back of the sled, standing tall, waving my arms, and screaming as loud as I could at her, hoping she would take her calf and leave us alone. Well, my screaming and waving my arms did get her attention, but she didn't run off. Instead, it made her angrier. She ignored my dogs and charged past the team towards me, her hackles up, nostrils flaring. All I saw was the whites of her eyes. She was smacking her lips together, which I later learned from a wildlife biologist is a sign she was very angry. He said bears will do this as well.

I was dumbfounded that she would leave her calf next to my dogs and come at me. Well, I guess my dogs were smarter than I, as they chose to be perfectly quiet and not rile her up. I had a split second to make a decision, and my first thought was to get the dogs out of there, so I let go of the team and told them to go home. They were more than happy to leave; they were like, "See ya!" And off they went, heading for our cabin miles away. I stupidly thought I could run to a birch tree behind me, climb to safety, and wait until the moose calmed down and left. Then, I could walk those miles back to the cabin. Dumb idea! The snow was too deep, and moose can run very fast through deep snow as they have such long, spindly legs. She caught me halfway to the tree and rammed me. I fell back in the snow, and the last thing I remembered was her front hooves raining down on me. She knocked me unconscious and left me for dead.

Based on the time-lapse, we figure I was unconscious for about thirty minutes, which is dangerous, especially in those temperatures.

When I came to, I had no idea what happened or where I was. I just lay there motionless and in incredible pain as my mind started to clear. Then I remembered the moose and wondered if she was still here. *Was she watching me?* I tried not to move anything but my eyes to see if she was still around. It seemed she was gone, and it was eerily quiet. The pain in my right arm was excruciating, and as I tried to stand, I had trouble breathing. I would later discover that she had torn the cartilage in my sternum and broken some ribs. I also had a concussion. My right hand was swollen, which the surgeon figured meant I had tried to block her blows. Wildlife biologists say that if you are ever attacked by a wild animal, you should just play dead! Well, I would bet the wildlife biologists who say that have never been attacked by a wild animal themselves because I don't think it is humanly possible not to defend yourself. The intense pain in my right arm was from a fractured elbow that no doubt occurred when she first rammed me. The surgeon later told me the two bones had been pushed an inch and a half apart. I couldn't believe that was physiologically possible.

The snow being so deep may have actually helped save me because it acted as a cushion as she was stomping me, and when she was gone, it helped insulate my body. The locals later told me if she had caught me on the hard, packed trail, she would have ripped me to shreds.

But as I lay in the snow, the cobwebs started to clear, and I realized how dire the situation was. I recognized that my sleepiness and desire to just lay there meant I was hypothermic on top of the intense pain. Hypothermia, which results in decreased blood flow and decreased body temperature, is what people who "freeze to death" actually die from. With my concern for my dogs' safety alleviated since I'd gotten them out of harm's way, I now had no way to get home. I could not walk those miles back to the cabin with my injuries. I was having a hard time breathing, my chest hurt, and I wasn't thinking clearly (because of the concussion and the hyperthermia). I had no use of my left arm, and it hurt like hell. I started to realize there was a very good chance I was going to die there. My dogs were heading back to the cabin, but there was no one at the cabin to realize I was missing. My family was still back in Bucks County, and they weren't scheduled to arrive for a couple of weeks. Mary Jo and I tried to talk every day but with a four-hour time difference and both of us busy, we didn't always connect daily. By the time she figured out I was missing, I would most likely be dead. I focused on my family over four thousand miles away and realized I had to try and get up and get moving. If I just laid there, I would never wake up. My goal was to make it back to the main trail where maybe another dog musher, a snowmobiler, or even a trapper would find me. If I stayed where I was, there was a chance they'd still find me, but it was likely to take much longer to reach me three hundred yards back in the bush. I had to make it back to the main trail for my family's sake.

I was able to stumble back to the main trail, but every step took focus, and the pain was incredible. When I finally made it, I couldn't believe my eyes: there was my dog team! The last I saw them, my team was heading home. It turns out that as they were turning back onto the main trail, the sled tipped over, the snow hook fell out of the sled, caught in the snow, and stopped my team. The snow hook is like a boat anchor, and can be used like an emergency brake to hold a dog team for a short time. There were my dogs, quiet and scared as I was. Six dogs faced down the trail towards home, and the back two were a tangled mess facing the opposite way—I'm not sure how that happened.

It is simply amazing that the snow hook would fall out of the sled, catch on the snow, and hold my dog team there to literally save my life. The average speed of a good sled dog racing team is around twenty miles per hour. It can be very dangerous for a snow hook to fall out of the sled when a team is moving that fast. We even have a bungee cord in our sled to hold the snow hook securely and prevent it from accidentally slipping loose. I can't believe it fell loose—it is possible I had undone the snow hook from the bungee just before I let the team loose.

When I got to my dogs, they were pretty shaken up. They were happy to see me, but they were lying there really quietly. Now, I had to find a way to get the back two dogs untangled and correctly harnessed with the use of only one arm. My injured ribs and sternum made it almost impossible to bend over, and with a concussion, I wasn't thinking clearly. With my head clearly in a fog, I did something at that moment that I still think about. The team I had that day consisted of young dogs and yearlings that we had raised from birth. I never had to keep them on a leash, as they were used to running loose, and they listened so well. As puppies, we would take them for long walks in the forest loose, and as they got older, we would take them for long free runs. When we were heading for a training run, I would simply just turn them loose, and they would run to the dog truck. When we drove to Alaska, during that whole 4,200-mile drive, I would simply stop and let them run around loose for exercise and a potty break seven times a day. They were used to running loose.

But for some reason, instead of just unhooking the two dogs with the tangled harnesses and letting them follow us back to the cabin, which would have been an easy thing to do with one hand, I struggled to untangle those two dogs, get their harnesses on the right way, and hook them back into the team. It was an excruciatingly painful and very slow process, especially having to do everything with one arm and with such difficulty breathing. I just couldn't leave them behind.

A great thing about dogs is that they live in the moment. By the time I got everybody untangled and all aiming in the right direction, they weren't laying down scared and quiet anymore; they were barking, screaming, and jumping to go! At this moment, their enthusiasm and apparent forgetfulness of the recent past had created a new problem because the snow hook was still stuck in the frozen, hard-packed snow. I had to free up the snow hook so the dogs could bring me back to the cabin, where I could call for help. The dogs were straining to go, but I only had one arm, and that arm had to hold onto the sled when we took off, or I would be left behind. If I took my hand off the handlebar of the sled to reach down and pull the snow hook out of the frozen snowpack, the dogs would pull the sled out from under me, I would fall backward, and they would be heading back to the cabin without me. So I had to be creative. I managed to stand on a runner with one foot, hold onto the handlebar with my good arm, and kick the snow hook loose with my other foot. Once I got the snow hook loose, I had to use my boot to pick it up and flip it into the sled bag *while* the dogs were taking off. That is hard to do when you are healthy, let alone with all the injuries I had. It was pure luck I was able to pull that off.

Off we went. The dogs had had enough downtime that they were crazy and really flying home. I don't remember much about the trip back to the cabin as I was in and out of consciousness. It was difficult to negotiate curves with only one hand, and leaning into the turns was painful with my chest injuries. Every once in a while, we would hit a bump in the trail, and the pain was almost unbearable, but I was able to hold on throughout it all. By the time we reached the cabin, I was in shock, and I really don't remember much of what happened at that point. I've learned from the people around me that my first call was not to get help for myself but to call our close friends and nearest neighbors, Eric and Stacy, to ask if they could come and take care of the dogs. Stacy came running across the slough that ran between our two cabins and up into our dog yard. When she got there, she was surprised to see that the dogs were all strung out nicely with a line to a snow hook in front to keep them from getting tangled and a snow hook at the back to keep them in place. I have virtually no recollection of doing any of that. Instinct must have taken over. She told me later that she'd thought if I was able to take such good care of the dogs after the run, how badly could I have been hurt?

My next call was to Harvey, another dear friend, to ask him to take me to the hospital. He came right over, helped me into his truck, and drove me forty miles to the hospital in Fairbanks. They determined I was in shock, had a badly injured arm, and breathing issues, and they took no chances. They immediately used surgical scissors to cut off my beautiful, and also very expensive, cold-weather parka. Good cold weather arctic gear doesn't come cheap. Harvey was horrified watching it—he later joked that if he knew they were going to cut off the parka, making it worthless, he would have just ripped it over my head when we were in the truck. He said I was so out of it I probably wouldn't have even felt it. Once the swelling receded, I ended up having two surgeries to fix my elbow, and they needed to use a stainless-steel bolt and wires to pull it back together. That hardware remains in my arm today, a daily reminder of the moose stomping I was lucky to survive. Post-surgery, I had to keep my elbow elevated when I slept. We lived in a new log cabin that we built, so to keep my elbow elevated, I would hook a long leash from the cross beam above our bed and snap a padded dog collar to it. I threaded my arm through the collar to hold my elbow above my head and keep it elevated. I was not allowed to travel back to Pennsylvania for six weeks, and even then, I wasn't allowed to handle dogs.

I had twenty-four dogs with me in Alaska the year I got stomped by the moose. I was in no shape to take care of my dogs or even myself for a while. Our friends Charlie and Terri really stepped up and took over my meal needs. I will be eternally grateful for their support. They established a "meals on wheels" for me. Friends brought me some amazing meals with halibut, salmon, moose, and caribou. Eric and Stacy stepped in and were there to help feed and care for my dogs. It was not an easy task, not knowing all their names or how much to feed. Our friends truly came to my aid; we will never forget that.

Mary Jo found a way to free up her schedule, take Alex out of school, and head to Alaska as quickly as she could to take care of me and the dogs. Sarah was in high school, so we decided she was old enough to stay home with her aunt and continue attending school. Mary Jo said it was an interesting experience to call Alex's school and explain that she had to take him out of school for a while to head to Alaska because I got stomped by a moose and was in the hospital, unable to care for myself or the dogs for a while. I am guessing that was an excuse that has never been heard by a school in Pennsylvania—ever.

People ask me if I am bitter about what happened with the moose. I am certainly not bitter; in retrospect, I don't blame the moose for what happened at all. She and her calf crossed in front of my dog team as we made the turn off the main trail. I didn't see her, even though the dogs did; that is why they backed off initially. Then we went around the big loop, and on the way back, we ran into her. In her mind, we passed her once but then turned around and came back at her. She saw it as an attack. She was just simply trying to protect her calf. That is what moms of most species would do to protect their young.

As you can imagine, the news spread quickly in the sled dog community about me being stomped by the moose. Especially concerning was the fact that she ignored my dog team right next to her calf to attack me. That freaked a lot of people out; they were worried something was wrong with this cow moose. I tried to keep the story out of the press. About a week before I got stomped, a young bull moose got tangled in some wires and became aggressive in a neighborhood in Fairbanks and had to be destroyed. That wasn't the first incident, and soon, there was a public outcry that moose were getting too aggressive around people. My story getting out would have only added to the hysteria. My attempts worked for about six weeks before the newspaper got the story, but at least with the story being six weeks old, it was no longer front-page material. Later on, a producer from a TV show about surviving wildlife attacks reached out to me to feature my story, but I politely declined.

The moose story follows me everywhere. In every talk or lecture I give, someone will ask, "Can you tell the moose story?" I have told it countless times, seemingly at every social event I attend. Once when I was at a wedding in South Philadelphia, I was asked to tell the story once again. When I was done, a little old Italian man shook my hand and said, "Man, I ain't never met anyone who got ever bitch slapped by a moose!" I still chuckle at that line! I guess people like to hear my story as many are intrigued by Alaska and not everyone has seen a moose up close. People's reactions to it are varied. Some say I am a badass for taking on a moose; others have called me "Mr. Rugged" for withstanding a wildlife attack. But really, I am neither; I just happened to be in the wrong place at the wrong time. Survival mode just took over—I think everyone has that survival mode buried somewhere. Luckily, most people never have to find out if they have it. Maybe I should have made better decisions. Clearly, my first mistake was not carrying a gun, something I corrected when I went back to Alaska the next year. I figured having a run-in with an angry moose the first time without having a gun was bad luck. If I have a run-in with a moose a second time and I still don't have a gun, I am a dumbass.

I went round and round about what kind of gun to carry. Most of my friends in Alaska carry a pistol, typically a .44 magnum, as they are easier to pack than a long gun. However, I work a lot with police canine units because of my background in working dogs, and they all said it would be difficult to safely stand on the back of my sled and shoot a charging moose with a pistol. They suggested getting a long gun, but my Alaskan friends told me pump or automatic shotguns or rifles tend to freeze up in winter. They said a single shot would be a good choice. I thought, *a single shot means just that: you get one shot! No*, I thought, *I need more than that*. I settled on a 12-gauge, double-barrel coach gun. A coach gun is the shortest shotgun you can legally purchase, and it fit in the sled perfectly. Luckily, I have never had to fire it, and it is back in the box I purchased it in twenty-five years ago.

Looking back, I also wonder if I had acted like my dogs and remained still and quiet, maybe the moose wouldn't have attacked me at all. Sending my lifeline—my dog team—home without me also wasn't too bright. But I never thought I would get beat up so badly I wouldn't be able to walk home to the cabin. Honestly, my dogs are like my family, and trying to keep them out of harm's way was a no-brainer. Faced with that decision again, I would have no doubt done the same thing to try and keep them safe. My lifelong passion for dogs was further enhanced by the fact that these dogs literally saved my life. I will never forget that. I'm not sure what your thoughts are on *help from above*, but I sense that someone up there was looking out for me that day.

PART 1

WHERE IT ALL STARTED

CHAPTER 1

Early Childhood Trauma

I grew up in the snow belt town of Ashtabula, Ohio, about fifty-five miles east of Cleveland, on the shores of Lake Erie. I am proud to be from Northeast Ohio, an area known for its residents' great work ethic. LeBron James, who also grew up there, said it best: "In Northeast Ohio, nothing is given. Everything is earned. You work for what you have."

I have been fortunate to live a remarkable life. The adventures that I have been lucky enough to enjoy or even survive have been a constant source of entertainment for my family. I would come home with these stories, and my sisters kept saying you must write a book! I just never seemed to get around to it; something constantly got in the way, and there was always another new adventure.

But deep down, I knew I could not start writing a book about my life without addressing something that happened to me as a young child. I grew up with anger issues and a complete lack of trust in other people. To this day, I still have trouble trusting people. When we go to a restaurant, I like to sit at a table with my back to the wall. I have an amazing wife, and truly, I am the luckiest man in the world. Life hasn't always been easy for Mary Jo; I know I have been tough to live with. Anger and trust issues can certainly lead to difficult times in a marriage, but Mary Jo was always so patient and understanding. She was also always pushing me to get professional help. I think she could tell I was hiding something. I was always making excuses for why I didn't get help—early on, we couldn't afford it, and later on, we were always too busy.

It really got to a breaking point, and one day, after another angry outburst that bordered on rage, I just lost it and started crying uncontrollably. I will never forget her holding me in her arms, telling me everything would be alright. I finally came clean and told her that when I was a young child, I was sexually abused by a distant adopted family member. This was something I had held in all my life—feelings of shame and guilt consumed me. I had kept this locked up inside of me, and I knew she was the only one I could tell. She deserved to know; it wasn't fair to her. That is when I knew it was time to get professional help.

The first doctor I saw was great, but when he realized after testing that I was suffering from PTSD (Post Traumatic Stress Disorder), it was clear that I needed to see someone trained specifically to deal with it. Anything above a certain score on the test I took was an indication you suffered from PTSD—I almost doubled that score. I was in total shock when he said this. It was hard for me to comprehend. I grew up during the Vietnam era when the PTSD diagnosis began. Aware of PTSD, I always associated it with veterans affected by the horrors of war. My brother served in Vietnam, as did a couple of older friends, and it seemed some of them came back a little different. One of my older friends had grown up hunting, but when he came home, he didn't want to touch another gun. These brave men and women who served our country are true heroes and deserve all the help we can give.

The treatment I received is called *exposure therapy*. This type of intervention helps people face and control their fears by exposing them to the traumatic memory they experienced in the context of a safe environment. The goal is to help you become less sensitive over time. This may be the toughest thing I have ever done. At times, I thought I just couldn't do it! Mary Jo was always there for me, encouraging me to stay with it. Every week, my doctor would push me a little farther, pulling back the curtain little by little. First, he asked me to talk about it; then, eventually, he asked me to write about it. Telling my daughter, Sarah, and son, Alex, was especially tough. You want your kids to think of you as strong and confident. It is very hard to let them see you in such a vulnerable position. I fought back tears as they did, baring my soul about something that happened to me back when I was a child. I didn't go into details—I didn't have to; they could see the pain. I apologized to them for being such an overprotective parent as subconsciously, no doubt, I was trying to shield them from having something horrible happen to them as well.

I also had to tell my siblings what happened as that was part of my therapy—another tough situation. Every week, I would come home and tell Mary Jo, "*That is as far as I can go. I can't do the next step, I can't go any farther, I want to quit.*" But with great family support and my pride in never being a quitter, by the next week, I would be back, and my doctor would get me to do the next step. He was amazing!

Something my doctor told me really startled me; he said the PTSD was not strictly a result of the sexual abuse but also likely the result of a lifetime of silence about it.

One day, when I was a kid, I went to my best friend's house. I was having a tough day, and his mom could tell something was really bothering me. I kept saying everything was fine, but she wasn't buying it; she knew me too well. Finally, she took me aside, and I broke down. I opened up and told her about the abuse. I was standing there shaking and sobbing in their backyard while my friends were playing in the basement, unaware of what was going on. I couldn't believe I told her about it, but I also knew the abuse was wrong and had to stop. She immediately called my mom, and I was sent home. I remember walking home certainly rattled, but honestly, I felt a bit of relief that someone knew, and maybe it would stop. I remember getting a hug from my mom, but that was it. Nothing was ever discussed with me by my mom, and my dad never said a word—it was like it had never happened. They never talked to me about it. You need to remember it was a different time back then; these kinds of things were never discussed. I do know my abuser disappeared from our lives, never to be heard from and never to be spoken of again. Recently, I went through a family tree book with pictures of each family member to try and find him, as I remembered his name. He was nowhere to be found, as if he were scrubbed from the memory of the family. My dad was a small-town lawyer, and he had some clients that were pretty rough characters, especially scary to a small boy. They liked my dad and would do anything for him. I am now ashamed to think, but at the time, in my mind, I was sure these guys "took care of" my abuser, and he would never be able to hurt me or another little kid again. Maybe it was a defense mechanism to reassure me that he was gone and I would never have to worry about him in my life again.

This exposure therapy has worked wonders for me. I am now comfortable speaking about what happened. I no longer blame myself, and I am no longer ashamed or embarrassed. My doctor stressed to me the strength I showed by not allowing this abuse to continue and telling an adult about someone hurting me in ways I didn't understand. He said I was brave for doing something about it as a child and brave as an adult for facing my fears. Maybe I didn't need to write about this chapter in my life here, but if just one person reads it and decides to get help, it will be all worth it.

I really believe a big part of my passion and my love of animals, especially dogs, grew out of the sense that they provided a security blanket for me. They provided comfort, as I knew they would never hurt me. I could always trust them, and they were always there for me. They were my best friends growing up. I always had a dog with me—I still do.

CHAPTER 2

◆

Boots My First Dog

My mom and dad grew up during the Great Depression, and that no doubt had a tremendous effect on the rest of their lives. They say that many of the children who survived the depression years carried the scars of the time well into adulthood or even until they died. They tended to be very frugal, and many had a hard time throwing anything away, possibly out of fear that it may one day become useful or needed. So, while we always had dogs and cats around, they had to have a job. All the dogs we had while I was growing up were hunting dogs. All the cats had to be good mousers. They could be great pets as well, but that wasn't their primary purpose.

My dad believed having a dog or a cat strictly as a pet was a luxury. If you look back in history, he obviously wasn't the only one who felt this way. Many years ago in England, dogs that had a long tail, not cropped, were taxed as a luxury possession. All the hunting dogs had cropped tails so they wouldn't get tangled or bloodied in the briars. Another reason for "docking" was to promote proper hygiene, especially for long-haired dogs. Guard dogs also had their tails cropped to prevent an assailant from pulling the dog off during an attack. Terriers used to do a lot of their work underground, so keeping the tail cropped helped prevent damage. Growing up, we had German

Shorthaired Pointers and English Pointers for grouse and pheasant hunting. We always had a beagle around for rabbit hunting as well.

Snooker the Beagle, the first dog I remember

Until a family friend gave me a cocker spaniel-beagle mix puppy from the shelter, we never had a pet dog in our home. He was a cute little ball of fur, all black with white feet, so I named him Boots. He was the first non-working dog we had, and I was completely surprised that I had my own dog—my dad even seemed to approve of the idea. Maybe my parents were tired of me trying to bring home every stray dog I came across. My attempts to smuggle them in had never been successful.

Recently, as I was writing this book, I had a realization that really startled me. Boots *did* have a job, after all. He was my *therapy dog*. Of course, this was years before there was even such a thing as a "therapy dog." But my mom and dad knew if anything would help me through the trauma of sexual abuse, it would be a dog. While later in life, my sled dogs literally saved my life, I can't help but think maybe Boots did as well. I honestly got a little emotional when this all became so clear to me.

As a kid, I was obsessed with watching re-runs of an old TV show called *Sergeant Preston of the Yukon*. He was a proud member of the Royal Canadian Mounted Police. He had two faithful companions: Rex, his horse, and Yukon King, his faithful lead dog. *Sergeant Preston* told the story of the Royal Canadian Mounted Police and their sled dog team. Every Saturday morning, it came on, and I sat in front of our old black-and-white TV, watching their every adventure.

Sergeant Preston had a special bond with Yukon King that I always admired. Inspired by their missions, in the winter, I would take Boots out and have him pull my sled, an old flexible flyer sled that everyone had at the time. Living in the snow belt of northeastern Ohio, we frequently got lake effect snows. After the roads were cleared following a snowstorm, we would have tremendously high snowbanks along the roads, and Boots and I would explore—I was Sergeant Preston, and he was Yukon King. Little did I know just how big a part of my life sled dogs would play going forward.

Boots and I were inseparable. He was my best friend and my protector, and no one could raise a hand to me with Boots around, including my parents! Back in those days, discipline was handed out with a belt or the back of a hand—today, we'd say my parents were "old school," but that was how *all* parents were at that time. One time, a new kid moved into the neighborhood, and as often happens back in those days, we ended up getting into a fight in the front yard. We were wrestling around on the front lawn, and my mom came out to see what the commotion was. Well, Boots came out with her and jumped off the porch onto this kid's back—he wasn't about to let him get the best of me. I had to pull Boots off the neighbor, and we ended up becoming best friends for many years until he moved away again.

Ashtabula is located at the mouth of the Ashtabula River where it joins Lake Erie. The name is a Native term that means "River of many fish." A lot of my early youth was spent working with hunting dogs. My dad, as an avid hunter, joined with a few friends to start a shooting preserve where they had a kennel of German Shorthair Pointers trained for hunting pheasants. They would compete in field trials. As a family, we called it the "pheasant farm." I got to work with the young dogs and play with the puppies. I was in heaven! As I got older, I even got to exercise the dogs before hunting season started. Some of the clients who came out to the pheasant farm were not only interesting, but a couple had some fame.

Rocky Colavito, a six-time Major League Baseball All-Star and prolific home run hitter (he once hit four home runs in a game), used to come out to the farm on a regular basis. He and my dad became lifelong friends, and I remember getting Christmas cards from Rocky for many, many years. That man had some big biceps! My dad actually used him to scam us kids one time. At the farm, there was a big old chicken pen that needed to be removed. My dad told us that if we tore it down, removed all the chicken wire, pulled out all the fence posts, and filled in the holes with dirt, we could make it a baseball field, and Rocky Colavito would coach our little league baseball team. We couldn't believe our luck! I do remember wondering why we had to remove the chicken pen when there was a nice pasture next to it that would be a perfect baseball field. We were way too excited to realize that there was no way Rocky Colavito could coach our baseball team in the middle of the Cleveland Indians baseball season! I still chuckle, thinking about how naïve we were. So we did all the work and made it nice and smooth, but of course, he was unable to coach our team. I always wondered if he knew about it or if my dad just used his name. Years later when I asked my dad, he claimed not to remember anything about it, of course!

I learned a lot working with those hunting dogs, including an appreciation for the dogs' instincts. These dogs just wanted to hunt;

Rocky Colavito, with me (in the middle) and my brothers Patrick and Denny

they were *born* wanting to do it. I soon realized these dogs had a genetic predisposition to hunt. Dogs have been bred for generations to do a task, and they do it with unabated joy. I saw it later with my sled dogs—they were doing what they loved to do when they were out running in a team. I saw it with the Australian Cattle Dogs with whom we have had the pleasure of sharing our lives. They want to herd something; it doesn't matter if it is sheep, cattle, our kids, or even the vacuum cleaner! I have seen the same thing with border collies, as they love to herd. Many dogs need a job if you want them really to be happy and content in a home.

If you want a terrier in your home, you may have some holes dug in your flowerbeds. If you want a husky in your home, it may be hard to keep them secure because they love to run. If you want a Labrador Retriever, keep a tennis ball handy, as they love nothing more than retrieving. When looking for a dog for your family, you need to consider what the breed was originally bred for; it may make your choice simpler and your life easier.

The pheasant farm was located in Saybrook, OH, and it was a great outlet for me as a kid. I just loved wandering through the woods or the fields, often with a young German Shorthair by my side (at least, he was supposed to be at my side). Often, his hunting instincts took over, and he would wander ahead of me, occasionally flushing a grouse or a pheasant. Then I would call him back, and we would continue our adventure.

Kids have a great imagination, and I was no different. I loved exploring the woods at the pheasant farm. A series of dirt roads led to the farm, and as we got close, a sweeping curve rose to the left. The road along the woods was lined with big maple and oak trees. My dad would drop Boots and me off there, and we trekked about a hundred yards through the woods until we came to a steep hill. We hiked down to the valley floor, which was about fifty yards wide with a stream meandering through the middle. On the other side of the stream was a steep hill that went up to flat ground and more large maple and oak trees. I felt like an explorer, totally on my own in the woods. On the edge of the hill, looking over the valley, were some really thick vines that hung all the way down to the valley floor. They were about two inches thick, and I could easily hang from them and climb them as they were very strong.

One day, I brought a hatchet with me and cut the vine off about two feet above the ground. I could then grab the vine, walk back as far from the hill as I possibly could, and then run as fast as I could to the edge of the hill and jump! It was amazing! My vine swing would sweep me across the valley floor, pretty high up in the air, and then I would swing back and crash back into the side of the hill. I did that over and over until my arms got tired or my hands started to blister. Then, I would hike down to the valley floor and follow the stream to a small pool that was less than four feet wide and about three feet deep. In the summer, when it was hot, I would just sit in the pool and cool off for a while before we continued our "expedition!" by hiking upstream until we came to a road bridge. We would walk out to the road and head up to the farm where my dad was working. I thought I was the coolest kid in the world, exploring on my own, and no adult needed. I really loved doing that!

One time, when I was probably around eleven, Boots and I were hiking along the stream, and he jumped ahead of me, lurched, and grabbed a snake. He shook and killed it. Afterward, I showed the snake to an adult, and he told me it was a copperhead, one of the most poisonous snakes in our area. If Boots hadn't seen it, I would have likely stepped on it and could have been bitten. I have had a love of animals for as long as I can remember, but my experiences with dogs like Boots reinforced this feeling!

Years later, while I was home from college, I decided to ride out to the farm and see how it had changed. Well, for one thing, all the roads were paved. The woods really haven't changed much, but they have certainly shrunk! I can't believe the overall distance of our hiking trail turned out to be less than a mile long! Funny how big the world is around you when you are a little kid.

CHAPTER 3

❖

Tragic Toboggan Accident

I come from a typically large Irish Catholic family: there were eight of us, four boys and four girls. I was the seventh child and the youngest boy. As you can imagine, many of the clothes I wore were hand-me-downs from my older brothers. Often, by the time I got them, some were a little threadbare. One time, I did something to one of my brothers; as I tried to run away from him, he grabbed at the back of my pajamas, and I simply ran out the front of them! They tore right off, like a tear-away jersey.

We lived on the shores of Lake Erie, which certainly was a big part of our life. We would walk to the beach in the summer and hang out or walk out on the break wall that ran all the way out to the lighthouse and fish for perch. We also used to play on the banks that led down to the lake. It was pretty steep and overgrown with brush and scrub trees. In other areas, it was more open—a combination of sand, clay, and rocks. We even found a hollowed-out opening way up on the bank. As kids, we were told that it used to be a tunnel that was part of the Underground Railroad. I have never been able to find out if that was true about that specific location, but Ashtabula was indeed part of the underground railroad, and the Hubbard House in

Ashtabula Harbor was a historic "last stop" on the trip to freedom for many slaves who fled to freedom in Canada.

It was a different time when we were growing up; I think kids were left to their own devices more. Or maybe it was that way specifically for me because, with that many kids, my parents may have been burned out watching them. By the time I came around, I was more on my own. I look back on it now and think I had a pretty good childhood. I had chores that had to be done, no questions asked. But after my chores were done, I had a lot of freedom. During the summers, we played baseball in a vacant lot two doors down on our street, and during the fall, we played football there. We picked our own teams and settled our own disputes about things like being safe or out or what the score was—all with no parents involved.

My dad got an old three-room canvas tent from a client who couldn't afford to pay his bill, so he gave my dad the tent instead. We had no air conditioning in our house, and my brother Patrick and I shared a room on the second floor that got unbearably hot in the summer. So the day school let out in the late spring, we would set up this canvas tent in the vacant lot and sleep in it every night until school started in the fall. It was great sleeping outside—most of the time. One night, though, we had a really bad rainstorm with high winds, and the tent started to leak pretty badly. My brother tried to wake me, or so he said! I was a sound sleeper, but I think he'd have woken me if he really tried. He went home to get out of the storm, and he left me in the tent. After he left, the water kept coming in, and the tent started to collapse under the weight of the water that was collecting on the roof of the tent. When I woke up in the morning, I was lying in two inches of water, and the tent ceiling was only about four inches above my head. I couldn't believe it. Boy, did Patrick get in trouble for leaving me out there!

Other parents in the neighborhood were also not afraid of getting on you if you misbehaved. Your parents respected and appreciated that. My dad was old school in terms of discipline, and he expected us to behave and treat people with respect. I used to say I wasn't afraid of my teachers, I wasn't afraid of the police, but I was afraid of my dad. I worry that today, parents don't want to be parents; they want to be their kid's best friend. I loved coaching youth sports, but some parents have taken the fun out of it. The more decisions you let your kids make on their own, the more responsibility they are going to be able to handle. As Banksy said, "A lot of parents will do anything for their kids except let them be themselves."

In the winter, that hill leading down to Lake Erie also made for an amazing toboggan ride. The hill descends steeply for about seventy-five yards until it flattens out on the beach, so we had plenty of room to slow down to a stop. My older siblings and their friends used to go tobogganing down the hill all the time. My next oldest brother, Denny, and I were always too young to go with them. But one day, when Denny was nine, and I was six, we stood in the kitchen while the older kids were getting ready to go sledding, and Denny just kept begging my mom to let him go. He was relentless. She finally gave in and let him go. The story I remember hearing was that he was so small that he kept getting bounced out of the toboggan halfway down the hill, so he was missing half the fun. They said he started wrapping his feet in the ropes that ran down the side of the toboggan to hold onto. On one of the runs, they went off trail and were heading straight for a tree stump, so everyone on the toboggan bailed off—except Denny. His feet were tangled in the ropes, and he couldn't get off before the toboggan rammed into the tree. Denny got launched headfirst into the tree stump. He lay there unconscious and bleeding from a severe head injury.

He was rushed to the hospital in an ambulance, and he lay in a coma for several days; his only sign of life was sometimes grabbing onto my dad's finger. The doctors did all they could, and he hung on but finally passed away a week later, on December 29th. To this day, I can't imagine the pain my mom suffered as she no doubt blamed herself. I was only six at the time, but two things I remember very clearly. One is that moment I stood in the kitchen with Denny badgering my mom to let him go, and then when she finally gave in and said, "Oh, go ahead, but be careful!" That has certainly affected me to this day. My kids learned early on that dad will never give in,

15

no means no. The other thing I remember so well from that time is us singing Christmas carols as a family a couple of days before the accident. My mom had such a great voice—she used to sing on the radio, but she really enjoyed singing at home as well. "Silent Night" is the song I remember most from that night. To this day, the first time I hear "Silent Night" during the Christmas season, I get emotional even though the accident happened more than sixty-three years ago. It made for a very tough Christmas; it was pretty quiet. I can't imagine what my mom and dad were going through. I am sure Christmas was the last thing on their minds, but they also had two little kids at home, so Santa still came. Denny's presents lay untouched under the tree as we silently opened ours. He lay in the hospital, with all of us hoping and praying he would pull through. Sadly, it wasn't to be. I have often thought that with the advances in today's medical care, he could have survived today.

CHAPTER 4

◆

Go North, Young Man

When I was young, like many high schoolers, I had several colleges on my wish list, but my grades were certainly not bringing in a lot of scholarship money. I also knew our family finances were not going to allow me to afford most colleges. All my daydreaming came to a sudden end when my Dad told me I had two choices for college. I could stay home, get my haircut, and go to the Ashtabula branch of Kent State. Or I could move to the Iron Range of northern Minnesota and live with my sister, who had just moved up there and was looking for some company, and I could go to a small community college nearby. I thought maybe it was time to spread my wings. This decision changed all aspects of my life and brought me to where I am today.

The move didn't start out so well. It was a commuter college with a small enrollment, and the student population was very cliquey. In the student union, all the kids from these small Iron Range towns would sit at separate tables, each one representing one of the small towns. One table would be all the kids from Eveleth, and another table would be all the kids from Cook, and so on and so on. But there certainly was no table for kids from Ashtabula. So, it wasn't long before my sister wasn't the only lonely one in the house. I didn't have much to do, so one weekend, my brother-in-law and I went to a sled dog race in Ely, Minnesota, which at the time was one of the biggest sled dog races in the lower 48. In fact, it was even a prize on *The Newlywed Game*, a popular TV show in the early '70s. The prize was an all-expense paid trip to the Ely Sled Dog Championships!

As someone with such a love of dogs, there is nothing I enjoy more than watching a dog delight in doing what he has been bred to do. Attending this race was amazing for me. I was hooked, and I realized *this* was what I wanted to do when I grew up (something I think many of my family members are still patiently waiting for!). I started to accumulate castoffs and misfit sled dogs. I focused on dogs with behavior problems, which I had hoped to fix or at least learn to tolerate. If a dog was too slow, there wasn't much I could do about that, as it is a physiological limitation. However, I felt I could fix many behavior problems. Besides, I identified with misfits. I felt I never fit in with people, but I was good with animals.

I know it may be hard for some people to truly understand the bond that can occur between a person and a dog. But a dog can read you so well. Sometimes, you don't even need to speak to them, yet they know what you want. The bond you can develop is truly something special. Dogs are also good at reading your moods: when I am having a bad day, my dogs know it, and they give me plenty of space. When I am excited, they get excited as well. Dogs pay attention to a variety of signals and notice how their human partners are feeling. Dogs watch humans for cues, can recognize changes in facial expressions and behaviors, and can even pick up on chemical changes in our bodies by using their incredible sense of smell. An emotional change in humans activates chemical changes that dogs can detect, and eventually, they learn to equate certain scents to specific emotions. I have also always believed that a dog is a good judge of character. When someone comes around, and my dog is wary of them, I take the warning not to trust that person immediately. For example, one season in Alaska, we had a dog musher rent a cabin near where we lived to train and race his dogs for the season. My dogs just didn't like him. If he came walking down our driveway, which was about a quarter-mile long, I could tell by the tone of their bark it was him without even looking.

You can train a dog to do almost anything; it is really amazing. You can train almost any dog to take commands, but a good leader must be born with some innate ability. Of course, you need to instill confidence in them and be able to bring out the best in them. Not everyone can train dogs; I think patience and consistency are the most important attributes needed. We gave every dog a chance to run in lead, because some will surprise you. One year, we had a litter of just two puppies—both coal-black females—and we named them Pitch and Tar. They looked identical, but their personalities were as different as day and night. Pitch was a shy dog that seemed to be afraid of everything. Tar was the complete opposite, friendly as can be and afraid of nothing. If you didn't know better, you would find it hard to believe they were raised side-by-side in the same environment. They both got their chance to run in lead, and Tar said *no thanks.* She was completely fine running in the team. But Pitch, who was so shy at other times, seemed to thrive in lead. She was like a different dog up there. It was like she put on her superhero cape and was transformed.

As with many dog people, I think Mary Jo and I both have a way with dogs. I was visiting a friend at his veterinary practice, and he wanted to show me the young bird dog he had with him that day in the clinic. As we were walking back to the recovery room where his dog was, he warned me that the dog was protective of the cage he was in and would bark and growl at me. Well, when I walked up to the dog, he was fine, and he even let me stick my fingers through the bars and scratch his neck. My friend couldn't believe it. Another time, I was visiting friends at their farm in Ohio, and they had an Australian cattle dog that would bite or heel anybody who came to visit. They always put their dog away whenever they had company. I told them to turn him loose; I was fine with it. He didn't hesitate, as I am sure he thought his heeler would nail me, and I would deserve it for being so sure of myself. Their dog came racing over to me, and I didn't move or flinch. Their heeler sniffed me but exhibited no aggression. We sat out on the lawn, enjoyed a beer, and a visit with old friends. Soon, the dog brought me a tennis ball to throw for him. The best way to most dogs' hearts is through food. For a heeler, the best way is to throw a ball or a stick, something they can bring back to you.

One dog who will always have a special place in the hearts of our family is a skinny, sickly little puppy from a Chester County animal shelter. Mary Jo and I were at New Bolton Center at the time, doing my graduate studies, and we went to a local animal shelter with a few friends who were young veterinary students. One wanted to adopt a kitten, so we all went to provide support. We were in great spirits, thinking about saving an unwanted and likely lonely kitten. It's not a good idea to have a bunch of animal-loving young adults go into an animal shelter. I think everyone left with a tear in their eye and a rescue dog or cat.

Mary Jo had her eye on a sickly little puppy in a pen with other puppies of various ages and sizes. He sat in the corner, looking off into space with a bit of drool hanging from his lower lip. The other puppies were jumping at the gate with excitement, looking for attention. I said that the puppy looked like he had a neurological problem. Mary Jo agreed. "Exactly! No one is going to adopt him, and in a week or two, he will most likely be euthanized," she said. I couldn't argue that, and I felt bad for him as well, so we adopted him. He was a skinny, sorry-looking little guy with a white coat and some feathering. We thought he was most likely some sort of small terrier mix. We brought him home, and he followed us everywhere, so Mary Jo named him Shadow. Although the name fit him perfectly, for some reason, I kept calling him "Smokey" (I still have no idea why!). Mary Jo soon realized it was going to be easier to train the puppy to learn a new name than to train me to use the right name, so Smokey he became! We also couldn't have been more wrong on our breed identification. He just kept growing and growing, and within a year, he looked more like an Anatolian Shepherd than a terrier. He showed no signs of any neurological issues and became a very active and healthy young dog.

Smokey was an amazing dog, for sure, but I guess we all think our dogs are special. At the time, we lived in an old stone farmhouse about three miles from New Bolton Center, and we used to ride our bikes to the campus with Smokey running loose right next to us. On hot summer days, he used to jump into a big pond next to the gravel road we were traversing, cool off, and catch back up with us. He was good with cats and other dogs, and he was good with people—that is, *adult* people. He just didn't like children. He would growl and even snap at any kid that came up to him. When friends came to visit us with their kids, we would have to lock Smokey up in a bedroom. When we left graduate school, he came with us to Minnesota and eventually back to Pennsylvania when we moved to Bucks County. As Smokey aged, he became a little more mellow, but his dislike of children remained strong.

Then Mary Jo got pregnant.

As the baby's due date got closer and closer, our concern for how Smokey was going to react to a baby in the house started to grow as well. Mary Jo didn't laugh when I suggested that maybe for the baby's safety, we put her up for adoption. I pointed out that Smokey did have seniority, and he was already a big part of the family. Of course, I was joking, but I wondered if Mary Jo thought so.

Well, the big day arrived, and we welcomed Sarah Rae into the family. We brought her home from the hospital, and Smokey wagged his tail as we came into the house. We cautiously brought Smokey over to meet her. I had a good grip on him as I let him get closer and eventually sniff the baby. He immediately warmed up to her, and it was like an instant bond was formed between the two, one that would last for the rest of his life. I was shocked! Mary Jo and I looked at each other in utter amazement! He was like a different dog—like we flipped a switch. He even started spending many nights sleeping by her crib. He was not only good with Sarah but with all other kids from that point on! He never left Sarah's side for the rest of his life. When she was young, we would play hide and seek in the woods, and it was easy to find her. All I would have to do was look for Smokey. If she hid behind a big tree, he would be standing there staring at her and wagging his tail. I wouldn't be able to see her, but it was easy to see a big white dog among the tall ash and maple trees. Another time, we were having a birthday party for Sarah, and all the little girls were out in the front yard playing a game of musical chairs. They were going round and round, and Smokey walked right behind Sarah in the middle of a line of girls. Mary Jo and I certainly got a chuckle out of that.

Sarah and Smokey, BFFs

Smokey had a long, wonderful life. But as he reached his mid-teens, he started to slow down. We knew the day that he would no longer be with us was coming. It was really a tough day for all of us when he passed, but especially difficult for Sarah, who was only eight at the time. She lost her constant companion, who had been by her side since the day she came home from the hospital.

My ability to relate to dogs helped me to work with several rescues over the years. My first rescue sled dog was a purebred Siberian husky named Nancy, whose owner thought she just didn't want to be a sled dog. I quickly learned that Nancy actually did enjoy running, but her previous owner was too demanding and too hard on her. Nancy was sensitive and just needed positive reinforcement. She really blossomed over the next few months and became a different dog. The next year, she was on my team, and we came back to Ely—this time as a competitor. We beat the guy who gave Nancy to me in the first place. He refused to believe it was the same dog.

On the other end of the spectrum was a big male husky we rescued named Founder, who was on his way to the shelter to be euthanized because of his fighting and nasty attitude—and boy, did he like to fight! When I rescued him, he had only half an ear on one side of his head and three-quarters of an ear on the other side. He had scars all over his face. At races, he created quite a scene. When it was time to harness him, he began snarling and growling, stomping around stiff-legged with his back arched and his hackles up! The noise he made was pretty impressive, and he scared many spectators—not to mention other racers. He reminded me of a football player before a game, slamming his forearm into a locker to get ready for a big game. I will admit I was nervous the first time I saw this behavior, but he never once showed any aggression towards me. Dogs can read you so well—show fear, and they will pick up on it; show confidence, and they will see that as well. I have always said that dogs are a good judge of character. If someone comes around and my dogs don't like them, I become very wary of them as well.

The key for Founder to be an important part of our team was for me to channel that excitement and aggression to racing. He was a big, strong dog who had plenty of speed. I just had to find him a partner that he would tolerate and not intimidate to run with him in the team. It became obvious it had to be a female as he would want to fight any male I ran him next to. Any time you are hooking up a dog team, the excitement is amazing. These dogs just go crazy; they love running so much. But put them in a race, and the excitement increases exponentially. They know the difference between training and racing. Founder would get so excited that he would just jump any male I tried to run him with. He would also intimidate a passive female, and they would be hesitant to run with him. But put him with a dominant female, an alpha female, may I say *a bitch*, and she would put him in his place. He was a perfect gentleman. Another concern, however, was the possibility that a dog from another team would lean out and show aggression as we were passing them—that was a trigger for Founder, who would defend the honor of our whole team!

As a young college student, I had no money to buy dogs, so I relied on this habit of rescuing unwanted cast-offs, which were some of the best dogs I have ever owned. None of this would have happened without the support of my sister, Pat, and brother-in-law, Dick, who financed the operation and helped train and race the dogs.

That tradition continues today as Mary Jo and I are still rescuing dogs and cats. A few years ago, we adopted an eleven-year-old Australian Cattle Dog that Mary Jo saw on Instagram. Lacey's owner had gone to jail, and she was put in a foster home where she escaped and was on the lam for eighteen days before they trapped her. It looked like she lost parts of both ears to frostbite, probably when she was a little puppy. She had obviously had a tough life and was afraid of any noise or quick hand movement. It didn't take long for her to calm down at our house, though. She quickly never even needed to be on a leash, and she never thought about running off. She enjoyed jumping in our pool and going for a swim. A few months later, we also rescued Lee, a two-year-old Australian Cattle Dog who had already been returned to the animal shelter twice and placed in a foster home. He

Lee went from almost being euthanized to being featured in Pet Age Magazine *(2018)*
Photo credit: Bobby Kelly

was kicked out of the foster home and returned to the animal shelter, where they deemed him to be unadoptable, and he was scheduled to be euthanized. The cattle dog rescue found him, thought he was purebred, and decided someone should be able to handle him. They thought of those crazy sled dog people in PA who have had cattle dogs and should be able to handle him, so they sent him up to us.

I will admit for about the first five days we had him, Mary Jo and

I thought maybe the folks at the shelter were right! I finally had a breakthrough moment with him, and he has been great with us for the last seven years. He is fantastic with our kids and grandkids as well. We must be careful, as he is very protective of Mary Jo and me. It is like he thinks we saved him, so now it is his job to return the favor. When I take him to the office, he lays there, and if anyone tries to come in, Lee meets them at the door, sits down in front of them, and starts growling—he won't let them in until I say it is okay!

Australian Cattle Dogs are an interesting breed. Their origin can be traced back to Australia, where local herding dogs were crossed with a domesticated Australian dingo. Here is a breed that has been genetically selected to bully an animal forty times its own size, so they are pretty fearless. They move cattle by biting them in the heels, so they are also known as blue or red heelers, depending on the color of the dog. They can be tough and strong-willed, but they are intelligent and loyal, but they are not a breed for everyone.

We got our first cattle dog puppy from sled dog friends of ours in Alaska who always had a cattle dog around. They sometimes took her out on a snowmobile and turned her loose to harass a moose that wouldn't get off the dog trail and was leaving big holes along the trail as she meandered along. These holes left by a long-legged heavy moose can be really dangerous for a dog to step in. The moose finally decided to just head back to the woods rather than have this pesky little dog nipping at its heels. Our friend Roxy shipped us the puppy we named Mic, and she rode with me to Alaska in the cab of the truck for sixteen years. She was simply amazing. She never had a leash on her but listened perfectly and always stayed by our side. She was so protective of our kids. If we were hanging out as a family Mic was fine, but if it was just her and the kids, she became very watchful, feeling it was her job to protect the kids. Occasionally, when we were outside, and we had the puppies running around loose—especially when they got a little older and maybe didn't listen so well—we could just tell Mic to go get them. She would be off like a rocket, running down the puppies and herding them right back to us. They would come running back with their tails between their legs. They quickly learned that if Mic was around, they should listen very well.

Mic, our first heeler

On the drive to Alaska for a few years, there was some trouble with bison on the highway between Muncho Lake, BC, and Watson Lake, Yukon. The problem with bison is if you agitate them, they will often charge. So, if they are standing in the middle of the road, you should not beep your horn or flash your lights at them; just be patient until they move. Typically, you see bison in herds, as opposed to moose, which are usually solitary. So, a herd of bison can literally block the road. One year, when I grabbed fuel and a coffee in Coal River, they had a picture of a big bull hanging on the door that had been seen nearby—they had even named him and warned everyone that this bison was especially dangerous and would charge your truck if you bothered him at all.

Mic was in her element here. If we came upon a herd that was blocking the road, she started shaking with excitement, looking out the windshield at them—she was locked in. I would simply stop the truck and let her out. She would just tear into the herd, and like the parting of the Red Sea, they would simply move to the right or left side of the highway, leaving me a wide swath to drive through. I would drive past them and open my door, and Mic would come racing up and jump back into the truck. You could tell she was so proud of herself! As we pulled away, I would look back in the rearview mirror, and the bison were already congregating back on the road like nothing had ever happened. I would glance over at Mic, and I swear she was thinking can we turn around and do it again? She truly was an incredible dog, and we have had an Australian cattle dog around ever since.

American Bison, also called Buffalo

CHAPTER 5

My First Sled Dog Runs

I will never forget the first time I was preparing to run a dog team! When I started out with sled dogs as a young college kid alongside my brother-in-law, Dick, I was comfortable handling the crazy huskies I adopted as they weren't that different from the German Shorthair Pointers (GSP) I grew up handling. (The GSPs that we had when I was growing up were a lot different than the high-energy dogs you see today. The GSPs I grew up with were bigger and heavier-boned than their descendants, but then again, maybe it is just that I was much smaller back then.) However, I had no idea about running sled dogs. Usually, you start training sled dogs on dirt trails in the fall before the snow comes. On dirt, typically, you would train with some type of wheeled rig, usually three wheels with friction brakes. One of the advantages of youth is that you are willing to try anything, and you are pretty fearless. So rather than starting in the fall with our first sled dog team, when we'd have better control given the terrain conditions, Dick and I jumped in with both feet in the middle of winter.

We had a three-dog team, a sled, and harnesses, and I was excited to give it a try. My first attempts at training sled dogs certainly exposed my inexperience. My first run on a dog sled didn't exactly go as planned. We had put in a trail along an old logging road that ran along a ridge through some beautiful big pines and then down a slight hill where it opened up at a beautiful beaver pond that you would loop around before heading back home. In total, the trail was about three miles long. We pulled tires with an old Arctic Cat snowmobile to pack the trail.

Standing on those runners with the sled bouncing as the dogs were lunging, ready to go, I was certainly nervous the first time. Still, that adrenaline rush was something I felt every time I stood on the sled runners for the next thirty-eight years. Those three dogs were screaming with excitement, wanting to go. I pulled the quick release, and off we went. I felt like we were flying, sliding around corners, trying to keep the sled upright on the packed trail, trying to avoid the trees that we seemed to be flying past. I made it to the beaver pond, sailed around it, and we were now heading home. Well, on one of the final curves, my sled slid a little wide. I got too close to a pine tree, and one of the low-hanging branches knocked off my stocking cap.

I now look back and laugh at what I did next. I stopped the team, told them to stay, got off my sled, and started to walk back to grab my hat lying in the snow! Well, these dogs, bred for generations for their love to run, had *no* interest in waiting while I went to get my hat. They simply took off without me! Luckily, we were already headed back to the house. So, off went the dog team heading back home, and I was left on the trail to walk back home with my tail between my legs. I learned a very valuable lesson that day—never ever let go of the sled!

As you'll see, I learned a few valuable lessons the hard way over the years. In the fall of this first year in Minnesota, I used to hike out to the beaver pond, as I had never seen a beaver, let alone a beaver house, and I was really intrigued by them. However, in the fall, I couldn't get close to the beaver house as it was on the other side of the pond, and the land around it was too marshy to walk on. When winter hit, as was the norm, northern Minnesota got very cold, and ice on the lakes got pretty thick even before much snow fell. So, one day, I walked out to the pond, confident the ice would be safe enough to walk on. I brought my sister and brother-in-law's dog, Toby, with me—a young German Shorthair and Labrador Retriever cross they got for hunting. He was worthless as a hunting dog but was a wonderful pet! I brought a hatchet with me to check the thickness of the ice to make sure it was safe. I saw the ice was about five inches thick, so it was plenty safe. The pond was as smooth as glass, with about an inch of fresh snow covering it and not a single track anywhere to disturb the snow cover. I walked over to the beaver house as Toby raced around the pond, sniffing everywhere. I examined the house to see if I could detect any melted snow or frost on the top, as that is a sign of an active beaver house. They say if a beaver is living there, their body heat or their breathing will often melt some of the snow at the top.

Suddenly, the ice let loose, and down I went into the water! As I fell, I instinctively stuck my arms out to the side. I was up to my chest in the ice-cold water when my arms stopped my fall as they came down on thick ice on each side of my body. I was frantically trying to pull myself up and get a leg out on either side. Funny how survivor instinct just takes over—you are not thinking, just reacting. I knew one thing: I was in serious danger! It was about to get worse. Toby, from across the pond, heard the commotion and thought I was playing, no doubt. I let out a scream, and he came racing towards me. I thought, *My God, he is going to fall in with me, and we will both drown*! As he got closer, he definitely could sense my panic and was trying to stop, but now he was in a full slide. Looking back on it now, it was just like you see in the cartoons—a dog sliding across the ice. Luckily, he was able to stop. I would like to say that at this point, he reached down, grabbed me by the arm, and pulled me to safety, but that is what happens in the movies, not in real life. He said, *I am out of here*, and he ran the other way. I was thrashing around, struggling, trying to swing one leg up on the ice as quickly as I could because you don't have a lot of time when you fall through the ice. The weird thing, I thought, was that the ice was thick on either side of me. How had I fallen through?

With one final push, I was able to get one leg up on the solid ice and then the other. Then, I just rolled away from the open hole. I remember just lying there, breathing, trying to comprehend what just happened. I had to get up and get moving, as I was soaking wet, and it was only 10°F out. I had to walk back about a mile and a half to the house because I had no matches or lighter to start a fire to dry out. I went as fast as I could, my coveralls freezing stiff, making it hard to walk. I made it back, got out of my frozen clothes, and warmed up by the wood stove. Unfortunately, what I hadn't known before that day was that beavers keep a channel open in the water going to and from their house. As I got close to the beaver house, I must have been standing over the channel where the ice was too thin to hold me, and down I went. There was enough snow on the pond that I couldn't see the thin ice.

Outside of Alaska, the biggest sled dog racing circuits in the mid-1970s took place in Minnesota and New England. The circuit in Minnesota started in early January, but if you wanted to be competitive, you didn't wait until the snow started to fly to begin training. You would start in September when the temperature and the leaves started to fall. People would start training sled dog teams using a three-wheeled cart with steering and a brake. When Dick and I first started, we didn't have one, so I had to borrow something to use. Of course, this wasn't always convenient as it wasn't always available. So, I had the brilliant idea to hook my three dogs to the front of my bicycle. Wow, was that a ride! We flew down the quarter-mile driveway. I was able to slow them down enough to make a sharp sliding turn onto the gravel road, and off we went! I was thinking, *Wow, this is pretty cool, we are cruising!* Until we weren't. I quickly found out why it is not a good idea to train dog teams off the front of a bike: as we flew down this gravel road, a rabbit came out of the weeds along the edge and crossed right in front of the dog team. The dogs made a hard left and followed the rabbit into the ditch, pulling the bike out from under me. I bounced off the bike and went skidding down the gravel road face-first! Another blow to my ego, and certainly another *what was I thinking* moment! That was the last time I trained dogs off the front of a bike. From that point on, I borrowed a training rig from a friend who was also nice enough to help me out as a mentor.

*My first dog team with Wizard in lead, and
Nancy and Toby behind him*

Most of the time, when I ran sled dogs, I would have two dogs in lead, which is called a double lead. There is a lot of pressure running a single leader because they must make all the decisions and keep the team strung out and moving. Putting a second leader up front eases that pressure, and, theoretically, when you give a command, you double the chances of the lead getting it right. Of course, you could look at it from the other side and think, *now I have twice as many dogs that could get the command wrong*! Many dogs simply can't handle the pressure of running single lead.

Probably the biggest blunder I made that first year running dogs was the time I decided to put a female who was in heat (in estrus) in single lead, with four intact (sexually active) male dogs behind her.

I figured we would really be flying with those four boys chasing a female in season! I never thought she would stop running to be bred. In my defense, as a young boy growing up, I'd often found the feelings weren't mutual when I was interested in girls! I wasn't very successful as a ladies' man. So, I just assumed this female would just keep running from these boys, similar to what I had experienced my whole life. I thought this was going to be an amazing run! A little back story here may explain my naiveté. When I was born, my head was so big both my mom and dad thought I was hydrocephalic (water on the brain). Growing up with a bucket head and being the smallest kid in my class until high school was made worse by my close-cropped hair and big black glasses. I was certainly not a babe magnet when I was young (some of my friends might say I have never been). My nickname growing up was "Sherman," after the character from the *Mr. Peabody and Sherman* movie, as I very much resembled the popular cartoon character. Rather ironic that I was nicknamed after a cartoon character whose constant companion was a dog. While I finally had a growth spurt and caught up with my classmates as far as height, my head continued to grow as well. I cannot buy any hats off the shelf—even the hats that say "one size fits all" sit on the top of my head, looking foolish. I have to special order hats from a company that sells hats for big heads. In fact, many of the hats I purchase are embroidered on the inside rim—"for those who are cranially enhanced."

Anyway, back to what I thought would be an amazing training run. About a mile down the trail, my leader, Salt, a female who was in full-blown heat, slammed to a stop and flagged her tail to the side to be bred, and all hell broke loose as four male dogs were trying to breed her at the same time. She never did get bred as they all started to fight over her. It was an absolute mess, blood everywhere. To this day, it was probably the worst dog fight I have ever witnessed! We literally limped home that day—everybody, including myself, had a couple of puncture wounds. Boy, did I learn a valuable lesson—to this day, I still chuckle at my naiveté! Luckily, no one was hurt very badly. But I did wait until she was out of season before I resumed training with Salt.

CHAPTER 6

Salt, the Little Dynamo

S alt, that single leader in heat for that disastrous run, was a little white husky with piercing bright blue eyes. Many of the sled dogs we accumulated were castoffs, mostly because of behavior problems, but some had physical limitations as well. Salt fit that latter category, as she probably only weighed thirty-five pounds soaking wet, whereas most of the dogs she was running with weighed closer to fifty pounds. What she lacked in size, she made up for in heart and desire. In fact, it was her sheer craziness that her owner couldn't deal with, and this allowed him to make her available to me. She was born in a big kennel and lived with close to forty dogs. With that many dogs, you are training multiple teams per day. The teams are typically based on age and ability. You likely have your main race dogs training together in one team. You may have another team of young dogs, yearlings that were maybe a year away from being in the main team. The yearlings ran in teams with older retired leaders who were great at teaching them what being a sled dog was all about. Then, there was often a third team—mostly retirees—who still loved to run, but their racing days were often behind them. The problem with Salt was that she could never understand why she wasn't on every team that left the yard! When a team would leave the yard, and she wasn't part of it, she would just go crazy and try and ravage anything she could get a hold of. She would destroy stainless steel feed bowls; water buckets had no chance once she locked her jaws down on them. She would also attack her own doghouse in an attempt to tear it apart. Clearly, she could be very destructive; restraint was not a part of her DNA.

Salt, the little dynamo and finicky eater

Salt would often get loose and chase the team that went without her. I have no doubt that this instinct to run is why some huskies don't make the best house pets—they just love to run. We got Salt as a yearling because she was so obnoxious, but I liked that attitude and was happy to add her to my group of misfits. Her owner got fed up with her craziness, and because she was so small, he decided she wasn't worth the trouble. She was also a very finicky eater. Sled dogs will typically eat anything you put in front of them. To have a dog that just picks at her food can create a difficult situation in a kennel environment when other dogs see food just sitting there and become jealous.

I was only training one team, so her desire to be a part of every run wasn't a problem for me. Every time I would run a team, Salt would be in lead, and that kept her very happy. But I quickly learned she *had* to be in lead. If I tried to put her further back in the team, she would be crushed and start to take her disappointment out on the poor dog next to her. She might have been small, but she was a dynamo, and she was the boss. Every other dog I had was intimidated by her. I quickly learned the best thing for the whole team was to leave her in lead, where everyone was happier. She loved being in the front of the team—truly a natural leader. You can train a lot of dogs to be lead dogs, but a natural leader is born that way.

I have been asked many times which is my all-time favorite dog. I have been blessed with some amazing dogs throughout my life, but it is sort of like your kids—you don't have a favorite—you love them all. If I really had to choose, I would have to say Salt remains probably my favorite sled dog of all time. She lived a long and healthy life, finally passing just after her nineteenth birthday. Her portrait hangs in our conference room, along with the harness she wore during her career. Honestly, part of the reason we still have her harness is a reflection of how special she was. The harness never fit another dog—it was always too small! Sled dog harnesses were passed down just like clothes in a big family.

I have to say, one of the toughest days of my life was when Salt passed away, but her legacy lives on. After a long and illustrious career, I could write a whole book about Salt. When it came time for her to retire, I think she knew, as it was getting harder and harder for her to stay in front of the young dogs. A fast team can create pressure for the dog trying to run in the front as a lead dog. And as strong-willed and hardheaded as Salt was, we could see it was time for her to start taking it easy, and she certainly deserved that. But that didn't mean she was any less important to us. In her retirement, she moved into the house and went everywhere with me in the front seat of my truck. She might not have been able to run as fast, but she certainly didn't lose her determination. She just simply channeled it in other ways.

By the time she was retired, Mary Jo and I would start our sled dog racing season in northern Minnesota in Ely, Grand Rapids, and Bemidji, then work our way east racing in Ashland, WI, Kalkaska, MI, Saranac Lake, NY, and Laconia, NH, and then finish the season up in Canada in Kirkland, Quebec, North Bay, Ontario, and Winnipeg, Manitoba. Salt knew that when we were packing the truck, we were going to be gone for a while, and she was not going to be left at home. As Mary Jo and I carried bags and supplies we would need on the road for the next six to eight weeks, Salt would slip out of the house, jump in the cab of the truck, and lay on the bags behind the driver's seat that we'd just carried out. It was pretty comical; she would *not* be left at home! We would make her get out of the truck so we could pack more bags, but somehow, she always found her way back into the truck. She was a good traveling companion, and at races, she would become a great cheerleader for the next generation of sled dogs we were racing.

Salt and I connected when she was young, and we had a bond you don't get with all dogs. She seemed to know what I was thinking, and I always felt I knew what she was going to do next. A good lead dog can also cover up dumb mistakes by the musher. One of the all-time, stupidest things I did while leading a dog team happened while she was the lead on my team. Salt not only saved me from looking like a moron, she even made me look like a pretty good dog man.

I was living outside of Cook, Minnesota, at the time and training on the Little Fork River that flows north into Rainy River up near the Canadian border. There are long stretches of quiet water broken up by the occasional rapids here. The quiet water often freezes over and makes for beautiful, smooth dog trails. The Little Fork is lined with low banks, flat land, and a dense forest of spruce, pine, fir, aspen, and birch. When we reached one of the rapids, we cut a land portage around the rapids (which did not freeze over) in order to be safe for dog travel.

Salt was about five years old at the time, in her prime, and she and I were really connected. Anybody who has had that special bond with a dog knows what I am talking about. Some friends and I decided one day we were going to put together a combined dog team, with each of us adding two or three of our best dogs, sort of an all-star team. We decided I would run the team because Salt was going to be the lead dog, and she would not run for anybody but me. Hooking up the team was sheer pandemonium; it was chaotic, with all nine dogs screaming to go and all the other dogs from our kennels screaming from the sidelines. The sled must be tied off to prevent these overly excited dogs from taking off before everyone is hooked into the team. This tie-off is done with a quick release that will be pulled by the driver when the team is all ready to go.

Well, we finally had all nine dogs hooked up and ready to go, all screaming with excitement, jumping up and down, and leaning into their harnesses. I held onto the sled with one hand, my feet firmly planted on the runners. The quick release between my feet was pulled taut and straining under the pressure of nine dogs screaming to go. I reached down with my free hand and pulled on the quick release to release the team. But it wouldn't let go! I was pulling with all my strength, but it still stuck. It must have had ice built up around it.

This was taking far longer than usual, and the dogs were only getting crazier and crazier. Many of these dogs didn't know each other very well and I began to worry about a fight starting. In a moment of sheer desperation and stupidity, I committed the cardinal sin in sled dog racing: I let go of the sled! I took my hand off the sled and reached down with both hands to yank on the quick release. Off it came, and the dogs took off like a shot. I flipped over in the air because I was no longer holding onto the sled, and the dogs pulled it out from under me. I came down in the snow flat on my back, and there went our dog team with no one on the sled!

This is a driver's worst nightmare: a team loose with no driver. Our dogs were now in race mode, racing each other! Loose teams with no driver can be very dangerous for many reasons. They can get out onto a highway and get hit by a car, or a dog in the team might fall, and the team could keep going, dragging the poor dog. I can't believe I was so stupid to take both hands off the sled! My embarrassment and guilt over my mistake were made even worse because these weren't even all my dogs—some also belonged to my close friends.

I jumped up and whistled and screamed to Salt, happily leading this team that was soon to be going out of sight. She realized I wasn't on the sled and heard me whistling and calling to her, so she started to make a big arc to turn the dog team around in a big field. She brought the whole team safely back to where we were standing, with not even a single dog getting tangled up. My friends and I stood there in silence, having a hard time comprehending what we just saw. Sled dogs aren't like other dogs, who will come when called if they are trained well. With a team of sled dogs, things aren't so simple. Those nine dogs basically become a pack. Salt had been down that trail many times and she knew where she was going—she had some muscle memory about the run. Sprint dogs are not used to turning around in the middle of the trail, and they just love running as fast as they can. In the old days, a trap line dog team might be trained to turn around on command, or even maybe an Iditarod team, but this behavior is not in the wheelhouse of a lead dog in a sprint team.

Salt was in single lead, so she had eight dogs chasing her down the trail. I am sure everyone was thinking the same thing when they first took off: better fire up the snowmobile quickly and start chasing them down the trail. None of us expected to see them come back on their own. My friends were amazed that Salt would turn that whole team around and bring them back safely; no one even bothered to mention how stupid I was for taking my hands off the sled! Instead, I got credit for being an amazing dog trainer.

CHAPTER 7

❖

A Change in Plans

Many people know about my lifelong involvement with dogs and my racing career, but they often ask how that transitioned into my involvement in nutrition and research. It all started even before I met Mary Jo when I was first introduced to sled dogs and was putting together my first team. I had a beautiful black dog with tan markings on her legs and underbelly named Heidi. She was a long, leggy, athletic dog who came to me from a good friend in northern Minnesota. She was young and inexperienced but showed a lot of potential to be a leader. Salt was the perfect mentor for her because their personalities fit well together. Salt was the dominant one, while Heidi was more than comfortable playing second fiddle and letting Salt call the shots. Physically, they were quite the odd couple: Salt was this little white husky with piercing blue eyes, and Heidi was a long-legged black dog with brown eyes.

I had an amazing bond with Salt, and I was hoping to develop a similarly strong bond with Heidi. Running her next to Salt would help her learn her commands. In fact, it really became the best way to train a young lead dog: hook the young, inexperienced dog next to the older trained dog and let them learn by example. But I soon learned that dogs can sometimes pick up bad habits quicker from their running partners than good habits! You also have to be careful as the young dog could become too dependent on the old dog and not be able to function on their own. The older dog could become a crutch instead of a coach.

Heidi, who helped start me on my nutrition path
Photo credit: Ashtabula Star Beacon, 1977

Heidi's gait was smooth, and running seemed effortless and easy. Heidi was learning quickly from Salt and was developing her own confidence. She was enjoying her role as a leader. Then, one day, I noticed her gait was changing—it was shorter and choppier—and she just didn't look right while she was running. The next day was a beautiful, cold, crisp fall morning, so I planned to take the dogs out on another training run. All the dogs were barking with excitement as I prepared the team. I was in for a shock once we began, as Heidi was even worse than the day before–she hardly had any control over her hindquarters. She was barking with excitement, still wanting to go for a run, yet she was dragging her hindquarters behind her like

41

they were paralyzed! Of course, I freaked out, so I rushed Heidi to the veterinarian, and they began doing extensive tests on her. I honestly had never seen anything like this, and he said the same thing. He asked if I was sure she wasn't hit by a car as he was really perplexed. He said he would know more when all the tests came back.

Well, he finally called and gave me her diagnosis: a selenium deficiency. "Are you sure?" I asked. I was shocked to think that this was the result of a nutritional deficiency. *All the dogs are on the exact same diet; why wouldn't we see it in any other dog?* I wondered. (Remember, this was well before the internet, so I could not easily look this up on my own.) I knew selenium was considered an essential nutrient in dogs, so foods were required to contain a minimal amount to meet those requirements. The first thing I did was change the diet for all my dogs, and what a difference it made! Not only did Heidi get healthy, but she also performed better, and I noticed that the performance of the entire team improved. It really was eye-opening for me, and no doubt it became the "aha" moment that changed my life.

I knew that I wanted to spend the rest of my life studying the nutritional intricacies to make our pets live longer, healthier lives. Now that I had a purpose, I changed my major from pre-law (a major I'd chosen in an effort to follow in my dad's footsteps) and transferred to Ohio State University to major in animal science, where I would study canine nutrition in particular. It was a good decision, as I would have been a horrible lawyer. After studying canine nutrition for more than forty years, I now know Heidi was *not* selenium deficient. Looking back, I am not sure how he came up with that diagnosis, as she really didn't have many symptoms that would lead to a selenium problem. It is almost unheard of to see a dog with a selenium deficiency. I am now quite sure that Heidi was suffering from *exertional rhabdomyolysis,* which is a metabolic disease that affects athletic and working dogs. It is related to extreme muscle work to the point that the muscle cells are damaged.

I have often wondered what would have happened if Heidi's vet had just said he was not sure what was wrong with her and I should give her two weeks off. By then, she most likely would have been healthy, I would have gone back to training her and would not have been thinking about nutrition, and I would have most likely missed my "aha" moment! I imagine I would have stayed prelaw, never met Mary Jo, and would now probably be a burnt-out, miserable old lawyer! One thing is for sure: I would not have been able to continue to run sled dogs most of my adult life if that had been my life's path. Pursuing a career in canine nutrition allowed me to continue working with canine athletes. They became a tremendous research and development tool. Funny how things always seem to work out for me.

PART 2

GONE TO THE DOGS

CHAPTER 8

◆

OSU and Grad School

My advisor at Ohio State, Dr. William Tyznik, encouraged my interest in canine nutrition. In fact, he helped me develop an independent study program for one quarter (winter, of course). Back in those days, OSU used quarters, not semesters, as they do now. This allowed me to run dogs all winter and get college credit for it, which was great. For my study that quarter, I was looking at calcium supplementation for working dogs.

In my dog team for this study, I included a couple of wolf hybrids. I am not an advocate for wolf hybrids, and I am glad many states are banning them. But at the time, I happened to be providing a good home for a couple of nice dogs that needed one. Friskie was a six-year-old who was supposed to be half wolf, and she was a sweetheart. Butch was five years old, and I was told he was one-quarter wolf. They both looked the part: big and grey with long legs and incredibly strong jaws. We would give the dogs knuckle bones to help keep their teeth clean, and these two could crunch those bones surprisingly easily. The rest of our dogs would work on these bones for about a week, but those two could make them disappear in a day. Butch could be a bit surly at times, and his temperament sometimes seemed more wolf-like than Friskie's. On some days, neither had the drive we saw in our other huskies. It seemed they got bored with training, though they were always ready to race. When I first got them, I started to look up information on wolf hybrids and was surprised to come across an article that claimed they might start to revert to behaving wild when they get older—around six years. I couldn't help but wonder if their original owner had read the same thing. Of course, this was well before DNA testing was available, so I have no idea if they really were wolf hybrids, but they were different enough from the rest of my dogs both physically and behavior-wise that I didn't doubt it. They were fun to have around, too, and I enjoyed having them as part of our "pack."

Heidi and Salt in lead, wolf hybrids Friskie and Butch in point
Photo credit: Ashtabula Star Beacon, 1977

One day, I was back in Ashtabula for the winter, where I would train on a quiet dirt road on the border between Ohio and Pennsylvania. There were only a few houses we would pass on our training run. One of the houses was a problem, though, as five little toy poodles lived there, and they would come running across the yard to bark at my team as we went by. They seemed to be getting bolder over time, coming closer and closer to us. I was so proud of my team as they just ran by and ignored them. All my dogs, that is, except for Butch, who was way too interested in them. I could tell he just wanted one of those little dogs to come close to him. Well, one day, they crossed the ditch and ran onto the road. This was the moment Butch was waiting for: he just leaned out from the team, never breaking stride, and grabbed one of the toy poodles by the scruff of the neck and kept running down the road with that dog in his mouth—the little dog just yelping. I started hollering at him to let it go, and he finally dropped the dog after we went about fifty yards. It went screaming back to the house with his tail between his legs, and the other four all ran back in fear! That little dog was scared but luckily not hurt, and the group certainly learned a valuable lesson as they never came close to our dogs again. They would bark at us from the porch as we went by! It was the best outcome for us, as I could see these little dogs getting too bold, and I knew something like this was bound to happen.

Dr. Tyznik was a colleague and friend of Dr. David Kronfeld, a professor and head of the nutrition department at the University of Pennsylvania School of Veterinary Medicine. As I approached graduation, Tyznik suggested to Kronfeld that I would be a great candidate for a grad student position he was looking to fill. Dr. Kronfeld was invited out to OSU to give a lecture, and while there, he wanted to interview me as a candidate to conduct a canine nutrition and exercise study. After the interview, he told me he was basically hearing from only two types of candidates: one group were complete intellectuals—they thrived in academia but were not very experienced with dogs; the other group were complete dog people—put them in a lab, and they were completely lost. Kronfeld laughed and said I was his compromise selection. Maybe I wasn't a genius, but I loved dogs and knew my way around a lab.

Kronfeld took me on as his grad student, and I moved to the Philadelphia area to work with him. The eight-week study I did turned into seven years of post-graduate work in canine nutrition that included studies in exercise physiology as it relates to heat stress. Kronfeld, who was one of the world's leading veterinary nutritionists at the time, became my mentor and dear friend. One of my most cherished possessions is a copy of Dr. Kronfeld's book, *Vitamins & Mineral Supplementation for Dogs & Cats: A Monograph on Micronutrients.* He signed it, "Rob Downey, the dog's best friend, with my compliments and respect, David Kronfeld." Years later, he encouraged me to start Annamaet and even helped with our first formulations.

Dr. Kronfeld, my friend and mentor

Before I went to work with him, Kronfeld told me that he did not want a robot and that I was going to have to think for myself and work a lot on my own. That worked for me as I have always been more comfortable around animals than people. We would usually meet once a week in the conference room, typically on a Friday afternoon around 4:00 p.m., and he would open a couple of bottles of Pilsner Urquell, his beer of choice and the best pilsner in the world. We would discuss how the dogs were doing, how the classwork was progressing, and what went on with the study during the week, all while sipping a cold beer or two. It really was a wonderful seven years. Interestingly, a few years later while in the Czech Republic visiting friends and business colleagues, Petr and children Lukáš and Lucie, we visited and toured the Pilsner Urquell brewery in Pilsen. This is the only place Pilsner Urquell is brewed in the world.

Kronfeld was truly one of the most brilliant men I have ever met. I used to attend rounds with him at the veterinary teaching hospital, and boy, could he be tough on the veterinary students. Many I became friends with, and some would ask, how can you work with that man? Some interpreted his behavior as mean and nasty. I saw the other side—a man who really cared and would push his students to be better. Years later, I ran into some of those students who were now practicing veterinarians. We always share a laugh as they would say, *"Now I get it; now I understand what he was doing."* What he was doing was going to make them better veterinarians.

Among all the opportunities that opened up for me during my studies at Penn, the best thing to happen was meeting Mary Jo. For me, it was love at first sight. She was so beautiful and so sweet. She was just natural and normal and so strong, a breath of fresh air. We dated for about eighteen months. But I think we both knew that at this point in our lives, this wasn't going to last. She was too young, and I was too immature. When she graduated, she took a position out of state, and I continued with my graduate studies. We were still friends and stayed in contact. Mary Jo's mom would send her any articles she read that included me. I didn't know it at the time, but I had a real fan in Mary Jo's mom. One of her sisters told me years later that the first time their mom met me, she told her that I was the man Mary Jo would marry.

We had both moved on with our lives, but a few years later, I was looking for a new certified technician to help with our studies. It just so happened that Mary Jo was looking to move back to PA, and she applied for the position. Anyone applying to be a new technician would have to meet certain criteria for education and training and go through an interview process. But ultimately, anyone I was considering for the position had to pass one ultimate test. I would take them out to the dog yard and watch how the dogs reacted to them. Because their most important responsibility would be working with the dogs, so it was critical for the dogs to like them. The dogs make the final decision. Of course, they loved Mary Jo, and I was certainly happy to have her back in my life. Our relationship grew from there, and soon, we were dating again and falling in love. We have now been married for more than forty years, and I can't imagine life without her. Funny how we now even think so much alike. I will be on the road and start thinking, *I should call her*, and then my phone rings, and it is Mary Jo!

Mary Jo has always had a special way with animals—always a calming influence. When she worked for Dr. Kronfeld and me during our studies, I remember whenever Dr. Kronfeld had to examine one of our dogs, give a vaccine, trim nails, or even draw blood, he always wanted Mary Jo to handle the dog. He always felt she had a calming influence on them, which in turn made his job much easier when examining the animal. Honestly, I can't help but think that her patience and the calmness she exuded with the dogs also helped us get through some of the tough times we had early in our marriage when I was struggling with PTSD.

The University of Pennsylvania School of Veterinary Medicine, now called Penn Vet, has two campuses: the campus devoted to the study of small animals is in West Philadelphia, and the large animal studies, the internationally renowned New Bolton Center, is in Kennett Square, PA. When Dr. Kronfeld asked me to join him there, we had a big problem. We needed open space and more room to do the work we had planned, which wasn't available at the companion animal hospital in Philadelphia. Our problem was that New Bolton Center was considered a facility for large animals only, and there were rules against doing any work with dogs there. We had to get permission from the dean to keep our dogs out in beautiful Chester County at New Bolton.

Early on in my time as a graduate student at Penn Vet, Dr. Kronfeld would send me to Philadelphia to give lectures to the young veterinary students on nutrition and heat stress in canine athletes and working dogs as part of the work we were doing. One year, I brought in Salt and a young Siberian husky, Bryer, as part of my lecture to show the evolution of body type in working dogs. Bryer wasn't even our dog; we were keeping her for a friend who bred and raced Siberian huskies and lived in New Hampshire. Bryer was about ten months old at the time. The traditional Siberian husky was becoming more popular as a show dog than a working dog and the top sled dogs had become Alaskan huskies. Alaskan huskies were developed in the villages of Alaska more for their working ability than for pretty blue eyes or a fluffy tail.

At the time, I drove a nice pickup truck with a set of dog boxes on the back that could comfortably and safely carry eight dogs. After my lecture that day, Kronfeld asked me if I could help him get his son's car started three blocks from campus. His son was attending Penn at the time. I went over and gave him a jump, but he soon flooded the engine. Engine flooding was a common problem back then with carbureted cars, but newer fuel-injected ones are immune to the problem. These engines became widely used by the 1990s, so you may have never even heard of this happening if you weren't driving before then. Flooding would occur most often during starting, especially under cold conditions, or because the accelerator has been pumped. You just need to let the car sit for a while if this happens, and then try to start it again later. So, we decided to go across the street to a restaurant, get some dinner, and let the car sit for a while.

Upon leaving the restaurant, my heart sank and panic set in as I looked at my truck and saw that someone had stolen the two dogs. Both Salt and Bryer were gone! How did I know they were stolen and didn't just get loose? Each dog box has fresh straw for bedding, and when a dog jumps out of the box willingly, he pushes the straw to the back of the box as he comes out. If a dog doesn't want to come out, he will plant his feet, which drags everything out of the box with him. There was straw all over the street, which told me someone dragged them out of the truck! Whoever took them was pretty bold, as both dogs obviously didn't want to go!

I was in a panic, and Kronfeld felt horrible as well. All I wanted to do was to get my dogs back. Because they were basically part of the university, all the local Philadelphia networks picked up on this story about the University of Pennsylvania research dogs being stolen! Of course, this was before the internet, cable TV, or cell phones, so "all the networks" consisted of ABC, CBS, and NBC. They covered this story almost every day as we searched for the stolen dogs. I did crazy things, like calling for my dogs as I walked down a fence line while they filmed me. This went on for two weeks. I was all over the news. Frankly, it was very embarrassing to have these cameras in my face as I was calling the dogs, but honestly, I would do anything to help me get these dogs back. I felt awful that I'd lost them, especially when one of them wasn't even mine and the other was my beloved Salt. I couldn't sleep. I didn't want to eat. All I could do was think, *Where could they possibly be? Are they alright? Are they even alive?*

We got calls daily from people who claimed they had my dogs. Many were just looking for the reward. We were constantly checking the shelters. The Philadelphia police were a great help—carrying out the search and instructing me on how to search for myself in a safe manner. These were good reminders, as I was a little out of my mind trying to get these dogs back, and I would go anywhere to meet anyone if I thought it would bring them home. I quickly realized that some of these people weren't to be trusted. They were just looking to rob me of the cash reward.

The university was also involved. They told me that if someone had my dog, I was to pay the reward we offered. No questions asked, and don't put up a struggle. They didn't want any trouble. After a few days we finally got a solid call on Bryer. Someone called and said they had her, gave an accurate description of her, and I was convinced this tip was legitimate. They wanted to meet me in some back alley where we could do the exchange, but I was weary of this arrangement. We had so many false claims about having my dogs that I didn't trust anyone by this point. I certainly wasn't going to meet someone in a back alley when they knew I would be carrying $250 cash. So, I told him I would meet him on the corner of Walnut and 34th Street at noon the next day. I knew he would be coming from the east, so he would be crossing 33rd Street, and I would be coming from the opposite direction. He would be walking a dog, hopefully Bryer, so I would be able to see the dog, but hopefully, he would not have any idea who I was. That is a busy intersection at noon, and there would be a lot of people crossing then, so I figured it would be safe. I certainly did not want to involve the police as I was afraid he wouldn't show. I told him if it was indeed my dog, I would hold up the cash in my right hand. I said we would meet in the middle of the intersection; I would take Bryer and hand him the cash, no questions asked.

When I arrived at the meeting point, I saw that he did really have Bryer. I was so excited to get her back!

Salt was still missing. One thing about Salt comforted me: she was my dog, and she would not be staying with any stranger if she had a chance to get away. I knew she would be trying to find me. She had never been good with strangers, and she wouldn't just go to anyone. However, she was stolen in West Philadelphia, and we were in Kennett Square, PA, about a forty-five-minute drive from Philadelphia, all through a busy metropolitan area. She was used to the woods and had never been in a big city before. She was raised in northern Minnesota, and she had only been on the East Coast for about a year. If she got loose and was trying to find me, she would have to cross the Schuylkill River to get home, and the bridges over the river had several lanes of heavy traffic in each direction. My fear was she would be hit by a car. Nowadays, I can hardly go to the store anymore without using Waze for directions. How would a dog have the ability to find their way home after riding to a strange location for the first time in the back of a truck, most likely sleeping and not paying attention? I tried to stay positive, but it was really hard. I was pretty much worthless at work, and some were even suggesting that maybe it was time to move on.

Trust me, that wasn't going to happen. I was never going to give up.

After about ten days, I got a call from a police department saying they had my dog—they had Salt! I couldn't believe it. Could it really be her? The description fit, but there are a lot of white huskies with blue eyes. But one way I would know for sure is that on the inside of her collar an *SS* was written in black magic marker—for the size of the collar—Super Small. They rolled the collar over to check, and sure enough, it was her! I got so excited. I said I would be right there, and then I hung up the phone! Only then did I realize I didn't know what police department had called me. No doubt the officer had identified himself and the station he was calling from, but I was so excited my mind went blank. I then had to wait for them to call me back so I could get an address. As I mentioned, the local news networks were great at keeping the story out there, and they asked if I would call if I got Salt back to let them know so they could film the reunion. One of my roommates remembered this and had the presence of mind to call all the networks. When I got to the police station, all three networks were there, and cameras were rolling to film the reunion. It was amazing to see Salt and how excited she was to see me. I was holding her so tight; then I started to cry, all the emotion coming out. I get emotional now just writing about it. But in retrospect, crying like a baby is not exactly something a twenty-two-year-old guy would want to be splashed all over every TV screen in the Philadelphia area!

The next day, I even got a call from the dean of the veterinary school saying I had done more to promote compassion towards animals in veterinary medicine than anything he had seen in a very long time! Of course, back on campus, my colleagues and friends weren't so forgiving—they bestowed upon me another nickname. I quickly became known as "Rob the Sob, I lost my dog, Downey"!

I really didn't care about the nickname, though, because I had my dog back! As it turned out, Salt got loose from whoever stole her and started making her way back to New Bolton Center. Somehow, she crossed the Schuylkill River and made it to Haverford Township, about twelve miles from where she was taken. She finally followed some young girl home who fed her. Someone who saw her with the dog recognized Salt as the dog everyone was looking for, and they called the local police. I never did meet the little girl, so she had no idea how grateful I was, but I did insist that the police give her the reward we had promised. I can't thank her enough.

Salt and I renited after a tough 10 days
Photo credit: Philadelphia Daily News

CHAPTER 9

Gig Racing while at New Bolton Center

W hile at New Bolton, we were able to train the dogs and attend races in the east. New Bolton Center is in Chester County, Pennsylvania—an area that is still horse country with a lot of open space and big farms. There was a nearby farm that maintained a large pack of foxhounds. Since Dr. Kronfeld was a member there, he was able to get me permission to train on their land. The property was beautiful, with trails traversing the rolling hills that seemed to go on forever and large grassy meadows with big oak shade trees dotting the landscape. These were some of the nicest, most picturesque trails I have ever been on outside of Alaska. Much of that area remains open space today managed by the National Lands Trust, thanks to the generosity of landowners whose thought processes were way ahead of their time. This area now includes thirty thousand acres of pristine forests, farmlands, and streams in southern Chester County.

Early on in my studies at Penn, I was training our dog teams in the fall on a forty-pound aluminum three-wheeled rig, with one bicycle wheel in the front and two in the back. As the driver, I would stand on a platform between the two back wheels with a T-bar steering control connected to the front wheel. There were friction brakes, one on each back wheel, activated by the driver pushing on a pedal to create the friction. The problem was if you had to get off the platform and, say, untangle a dog's harness, a small friction brake wasn't good at holding the team steady while you addressed the problem. These dogs are not good at standing around, so after about twenty or thirty seconds, they are raring to go. Honestly, they really don't care if you are on the rig or not. Standing at the front of the team with the leaders doesn't change much. They are going to take off, so you had better grab on!

I learned the hard way that this light of a rig could really only be driven safely with six dogs. One day, I went out with an eight-dog team for training. They were running well, and I was really excited. About halfway through the run, I stopped the team, locked the brake, and went up the team, praising each pair of dogs as I walked by. Of course, the dogs picked up on my excitement, so they started to get really excited as well. By the time I got to my leaders, they were really fired up. The whole team exploded, and off they went. . . with me still standing at the front of the team. I had taken too long, and they got too excited.

The team took off with that aluminum rig bouncing up and down, and it seemed the friction brake was doing nothing. As the dogs flew by, the rig was coming right at me, and I had one chance to grab on as it went by! I did and was instantly on the wrong end of an involuntary game of crack-the-whip. Both the rig and I were launched into the air, and, as they say, what goes up must come down! Down we came—the rig crashing down on its side and me crashing down through the middle of it. My right arm caught on the side bar of the rig. It was certainly painful, but at least the team stopped at the crash. I was able to stand the rig back up. The front wheel was bent, as was the T-bar steering, but I was able to ride the rig back to the truck with my right arm dangling at my side. I went to the emergency room. This time, I tore my bicep tendon, and they suggested surgery. The recovery time is very long, though, so I nixed that idea. I couldn't stand to be out of training for that long. I wore a sling for a couple of weeks and went back to training dogs as quickly as I could. Having a detached bicep looked a little weird for a while, but eventually, it healed itself well enough without surgery. My right bicep looked like it was in a permanently flexed position.

Many of the early races I competed in during the 1980s were dry land events where we competed on wheeled rigs with no snow. Many of these races took place in the mid-Atlantic states, from Virginia to New Jersey. I joined an organization called the Mid-Atlantic Sled Dog Racing Association (MASDRA), which had an entire championship season with a big banquet at the end of the year that everyone attended dressed to the nines. Many of the races had purses up to $2,000. Several of the top competitors spent their entire careers having never raced on snow. Plenty of them believed the MASDRA circuit was the top sled racing circuit in the U.S., Alaska be damned!

Over time, as Mary Jo and I accumulated more dogs, I started running bigger teams. Some days, I would foolishly run ten or twelve dogs in a team. The average size of the dog was between fifty and sixty pounds—that is a lot of power! I used to train one big team rather than two small teams because the temperatures in southeastern Pennsylvania limited the time I could spend training the teams. It would simply get too warm too early in the day, and it would be too hot to run the second team. So, I would hook them up all at once. I could train big teams on that light rig because, at that time, I was training dogs along the Chesapeake & Delaware Canal (C&D Canal) in Delaware. The dirt road that ran next to the canal had many power and light poles that I could tie off to for safety. I would carry with me a long, thick safety rope that I would use for this. I would simply tie the rope to one of the poles. I could then give the dogs a rest or switch some dogs around in the team. I had to be careful about what knot I tied, as it was always under a lot of pressure from a team of dogs, and I had to be able to release it quickly when needed. In other words, this would not be a good time to apply the "knife knot" because the only way to undo that knot is by cutting it loose with a knife!

I finally realized that for my own safety and that of the dogs, I needed to train with a heavier rig. May Jo and I got a new prototype from my friend Clyde—a three-wheeled rig that weighed about 350 pounds. The front tire was a large air-filled wheelbarrow tire. The back two wheels were from a Volkswagen Beetle that included disc brakes, so the rig even had a brake fluid reservoir. It had T-bar steering and a brake pedal similar to that of a car. A hydraulic lever was attached to the steering bar that allowed you to press the brake pedal and turn the hydraulic lever to lock the brakes. There was a trailer hitch welded to the front, so you could tow it to your training site easily. It was heavy enough that you could hook up a team of ten to sixteen dogs and maintain pretty good control. Clyde, a good friend of ours, started a sled dog equipment company called Risdon Rigs that continues to make some of the best equipment in the sport. Clyde would send us new sleds and harnesses each year to try because he knew how fussy I was and because he knew I would also be honest with him. They were great sponsors for our entire racing career.

Some of our early fall training was done on pastures, crop fields, and a small wooded area made up of tall oak and maple trees owned by the university. We would load the dogs into the truck and drive them a short distance over to a trail we put in that ran through a corn field to a pasture that contained a herd of Holstein dairy cows. At first, the cows didn't know what to think of these crazy barking dogs that would run around their pasture. After a while, they got used to us being there, and some of the young cows would even run alongside the dog team with the fence separating them.

Mary Jo and I parked the truck with the dogs out by the road. We hooked up the team by the truck and ran them on a tractor trail through the cornfield. After about a quarter of a mile, we would come to the fence where the cows would be watching us, wide-eyed. Our trail would make a ninety-degree turn to the right, and we would run along the fence line with the cows chasing us. Of course, the cows aren't as fast as the dogs, so we would quickly leave them in the dust, but it sure was funny watching them chase us. Eventually, the cows would recognize the sounds of hooking up the team, and they would all gather along the fence and watch for us to come towards them. Honestly, at first, I was pretty nervous running a team of dogs straight at the cows, only to turn as we got to them and run alongside them. What if the dogs didn't turn? What if they ran right through the fence to get the cows? That would not go over well with the dairy group at the university, many of whom, I suspect, were not happy about having a bunch of dogs on campus anyway. I was sure glad I had Salt as my lead dog in those moments because when I gave her the command to turn right, she turned on a dime. A couple of our younger dogs back in the team got yanked off their feet the first time, as they wanted to go straight for the cows. After a few runs, they got used to seeing the cows, but they never stopped watching them as we approached and made the turn to follow the trail. Occasionally, a young dog would look over his shoulder to see if they were still chasing us, but they never broke stride going around the corner.

By crisscrossing the corn fields and running around the cow pastures and through the woods a couple of times, I could get about a three-mile run for the dogs. This worked great in the early fall, as leaves started to change colors and temperatures started to drop at night while warming up quickly during the day. The training trail was less than a mile from the kennel, so the dogs weren't in the truck that long. I didn't have to worry about them getting too hot on the drive back in warmer temperatures. I would load the dogs before dawn and start down the trail with the team just as it was getting light and have them back at the kennel before the sun rose above the trees. Heat stress is always a concern when exercising dogs in warmer temperatures, especially early in the training season, before the dogs are in great shape. Simply put, a more conditioned dog will fare better in the heat.

This was a wonderful fall season—until it wasn't! One day in mid-September, while training for our second race season, we had some rain overnight. It was a little foggy and damp that morning when I went to train dogs. That day it was just me and the dogs as Mary Jo couldn't go with me. I was running the young dogs that day with two youngsters in lead. They had been around the trail enough times that they knew where they were going but they needed experience on their own as leads. When you are training young lead dogs, you can't just keep running them with older, well-trained lead dogs like Salt. The young dog will often just do whatever the older dog wants, literally following their lead. They may not even learn the commands as they don't really have to pay attention; they can just enjoy the run. So it is important for a young leader to be out in front of a team where he or she has to make the decisions. This helps build their confidence, but it also gives *you* confidence in their ability to lead your dog team.

The rig I was using that season had an expanded aluminum metal platform for the driver to stand on. Unfortunately, when wet, it was a bit slippery, and it was *wet* that morning. As I went around the first sharp turn, my left foot slipped off the platform and hit the front of the back tire while we were going pretty fast. My foot got literally sucked down under the front of the tire. I ran over my own foot! I fell backward but was able to grab onto the lower frame of the rig and frantically pushed down on the brake pedal with my hand to try and stop the team. The pain was excruciating but got even worse as I climbed back up and tried to yank my foot out from under the wheel. I almost blacked out. I was able to jerk my foot out from under the wheel but couldn't get it by the three-inch welded pipe that protected the front of the wheel. There was a small gap between the front of the tire and the pipe, and with the wheel spinning at this speed, when my boot hit the tire, it just got pulled right down through the gap. If the rig wasn't moving, I really don't think I could have fit my foot through that gap.

This was in the first quarter mile of our run, so the dogs were still crazy and full of energy. It is very difficult to stop a dog team just after takeoff, especially young dogs that are so excited to run. I couldn't pull my foot loose, no matter how hard I tried, and each time I tried, the pain was incredible. It was taking too long, the dogs started going crazy, and of course, it didn't help when the young cows on the other side of the fence started to run down along the trail, wondering why we weren't! While training on that trail, I usually enjoyed the interaction between the cows and my dog team, and I really think they both enjoyed it as well. But damn, I sure wished they weren't out that day! The dogs went crazy as if they weren't about to let those cows beat them to the end of the fence row. The dogs finally just exploded; they couldn't handle any more delay. They just took off with all their power—locked brakes be damned!

My foot, still just dangling there, got sucked under the wheel *again*. I was screaming from the pain, but also at the dogs to stop, pushing with everything I had on the brake. Boy, did I wish I had Salt in lead and my older dogs in the team at that moment, as they certainly would have listened better. Finally, I was able to get them to stop again, and I realized this may be my last chance. I was able to haul myself up onto the platform. Pulling with everything I had and fighting not to black out from the pain, I was finally able to pull my foot through that small gap between the tire and pipe. But now I had to make it all the way back to the truck with just one leg on the platform and the other leg swelling up like a balloon. I was trying to keep it from hitting the platform because of the pain. It was very hard to maintain my balance on one leg as I went around corners at a pretty good rate of speed. I was getting lightheaded and was afraid I was going to pass out and fall off the rig.

Eventually, we made it back to the truck. I was trying to collect my thoughts and consider what to do next. I wasn't thinking too clearly: I needed to get help and medical attention, but my first thought was to take care of the dogs. I could only stand on one leg, so I literally crawled along the team on my hands and knees, turning each dog loose to run back to the truck, as I certainly couldn't walk them back. This shows the connection we have always had with our dogs: I turned all ten loose from the team, and I didn't worry about them running back to get the cows or out on the road. I could trust them to return to the truck. I crawled back to the truck, took their harnesses off one by one, and hooked the dogs on small leashes we had around the truck. I got out the five-gallon water jug and gave them all a drink and treats. Then, I struggled out to the road and flagged down a car for help. As luck would have it, someone from the university who I knew stopped to help me. They went and got Mary Jo to take care of the dogs, and I was driven off to the emergency room.

My ankle was swollen so badly they couldn't even X-ray it for a couple of days. When they were finally able to take X-rays, it turned out I tore all the ligaments in my ankle and had a fracture as well. My knee was swollen from twisting while I struggled to pull my foot free, but I had no ligament damage or fractures. I was on crutches for several weeks, but Mary Jo did a great job training the dogs until I could get back on the rig. To this day, my ankle gets sore before it rains. They say this often happens because of a drop in barometric pressure that accompanies a storm that allows soft tissue and fluid around joints to enlarge, disturbing the nerves and creating pain at an old injury site. My ankle isn't much of a problem now, as I have had a few more serious injuries since then. The pre-storm pain now occurs also in both my knees, my right foot, my right elbow, and my lower back. As the pain is spread throughout my body, no one location is worse than any of the others.

CHAPTER 10

◆

A Break from Academia, Back to Minnesota

D r. Kronfeld had always encouraged me to keep training and competing with our sled dogs, even while doing my graduate studies. He always told me I could finish my studies any time, but the opportunity to race might not always be there. As it turned out, this advice was very personal to him. He was a Kiwi, and he told me that he had been part of a rowing team that was favored to win a medal in the Rome 1960 Summer Olympics for New Zealand. Prior to the games, a couple of his teammates were involved in a bad car accident, and they were unable to compete. This weighed heavily on his mind, as he never got this chance again. He wanted to make sure I got mine.

It was difficult to balance racing and my studies because my schedule was not sustainable. I had bitten off more than I could chew. I was running the study (certainly a full-time job), continuing my graduate course work (a major time commitment), and, if that wasn't enough, adding in training and caring for the dog team. It takes time to prepare for a racing season that will take us all over the upper Midwest and New England. Most of my days would start at 4:00 a.m. and finish up close to midnight. Looking back, it was obviously a brutal schedule, but at twenty-five years old, we all feel invincible. I lasted for about six months before I just wore down. My immune system weakened, and I got a cold. I didn't slow down, so then it developed into pneumonia, and before I knew it, I was in the hospital, unable to breathe, my chest burning. It felt like there were heavy weights sitting on it. I had a temperature of 104°F when I was admitted. I remember laying in the hospital bed late at night, soaking wet with sweat, burning up. I took a metal chair with me into the shower, where I just sat with the shower head wide open, with cold water only, trying to cool down. I was in a tough situation, and it was touch and go for a few days before I turned the corner and started to feel alive again.

While recovering one morning, an aide came into my room, said hello, unlocked my bed, and started to wheel me out of the room.

"Where are we going?" I asked.

"To surgery," the aide said.

"Surgery! For what?" I asked.

"To remove your anal fistula!" he replied.

"I don't think so," I said, "you'd better recheck my chart!"

He did, and it was a *whoops* moment that I will never forget. Nowadays, that certainly wouldn't happen with all the checks and balances in place at hospitals. That stay was over Halloween, and I remember a nurse coming into my room to get a blood sample dressed as a vampire, saying, "I want to suck your blood!" I got a good laugh out of it and told her, "I assume you are not doing pediatrics today!" I doubt that would be allowed today when everyone is so sensitive about everything.

This wasn't the first time in my life I fell victim to pneumonia. The first time, I was five years old, but while that was a serious illness as well, it was probably even harder for my parents than me. My sister remembers that my parents took me to the doctor, and I was in such rough shape he immediately sent me to the hospital. No doubt, my parents waited longer than they should have to take me to the doctor. Being their seventh child, they probably weren't in the rush that they would have been for the first or second child, and I can't say that

I blame them. I do remember the nurses coming in to draw blood or give me an injection because I didn't like the needles at all. I still don't. I have now had pneumonia six times in my life, and when I was younger, a doctor told me my lungs were pretty scarred from the infections. He said not only should I not smoke, but I should also not marry a smoker. He told me the scarring makes me susceptible to any respiratory illness I may encounter. No doubt he was right, as I have had pneumonia multiple times since and COVID at least twice.

The graduate work I did with Dr. Kronfeld has been published in various peer-reviewed veterinary and nutrition journals. The principal study we did showed you could increase stamina by 30 percent in running dogs by altering protein, fat, and carbohydrate levels in their diets. That work is cited in the National Research Council (NRC)'s *Nutrient Requirements for Dogs and Cats* (2001). It has been widely credited with forever changing the way modern performance and working dogs have been fed and has been the foundation for feeding sled, working, and field trial dogs for the past thirty-five years.

That seminal study showed the effect nutrition has on stamina. We also did some great work on heat stress, where we measured body temperatures when exercising dogs and showed the effects of heat stress on stamina. So, the natural extension of our work would be to complete the third leg of the triangle by tying these two studies together and taking a look at the nutritional effects on heat stress. We took this proposal to the company that was funding our research to get more money to continue our work. We were really excited about this next project. I gave a ninety-minute slide presentation in front of their technical service group, which included a few PhDs who had been following our work, and they were excited as well. Unfortunately, the head of their technical service department (who controlled the money) wasn't a trained scientist, and the proposal went right over his head. I always wondered how he got that position, as he had no training in the field. Well, he stood up at the conclusion of my presentation, and before I could even ask if there were any questions, he said, "If we want to sell food that will make dogs run cooler, we will just sell popsicles that you can stick up a dog's ass," and he walked out of the room! I was crushed. I was angry. The scientists in the room were embarrassed, and that ended the great work we were doing. We got no more funding. I guess he felt the money they were giving us was not going to translate into sales, so he put an end to it.

Amazingly, I ran into this jerk at a trade fair a few years later, and he was working for another pet food facility. By then, Annamaet Petfoods was up and running and doing really well. Lo and behold, this same guy comes walking into our booth with a big smile on his face, and he has no idea that I was the grad student he dissed so many years ago. Trust me, I remembered him. Then he proceeded to tell me why it would be such a great idea for me to move Annamaet's production to his facility, as they were so into quality ingredients, nutrition, and science. Initially, I was dumbfounded. Then I regained my composure and said, "We are doing just fine!" I thanked him for his time and sent him on his way.

My colleague, Kit, who was in the booth with me, was amazed I didn't say anything about what happened years ago and who I was. I just thought, *This isn't the time or place.* I remembered a quote that I try to live by: "Never sacrifice your class to get even with someone who has none. Let them have the gutter. You take the high road." Over the next few years, he moved to a couple of different pet food facilities, and he would always come by our booth at trade fairs to try to get our business. I never said a word about our past interactions, and honestly, looking back, I am glad I didn't. I was starting to feel sorry for him as he must have been having a hard time keeping a job. He always seemed to be with a new company.

By the end of my graduate work, Mary Jo and I had had enough of academia. I tried consulting on nutrition for a couple of pet food companies next. I made my recommendations based on sound nutritional principles, but I soon learned that unless my proposals improved the bottom line as well, the companies weren't really interested in what I had to contribute. I quickly realized that they really didn't care about my expertise; they just wanted to hear *their* opinion coming out of *my* mouth. That was very discouraging to me, and after a while, I realized that this was not going to be my future. Too many companies were being run by marketing people while the people involved in science and nutrition were being pushed to the side. My concern then—and now—is for the health and well-being of our pets. I had no interest in working with companies whose only concern was profit.

We needed a break from it all, so we decided to move to northern Minnesota to focus on working with our dogs. We had accumulated a pretty good group of sled dogs, and my sister and brother-in-law offered us their cabin on the shores of Lake Vermillion (outside of Cook, MN) for the winter. Lake Vermillion is the fifth largest lake in a state called "the land of 10,000 lakes." The surface area covers 40,000 acres, and it has been called one of the most scenic shorelines in the United States. It is also a great walleye fishing lake. The only problem with the cabin was that it wasn't winterized, so we had no running water. We had an outhouse for the bathroom, and for water, we cut a hole in the ice big enough to draw five-gallon buckets of water at a time. We would cover the hole with Styrofoam and then shovel snow on top to keep it from freezing over. The next-door neighbors were an old Finnish couple (Finlanders, as the locals like to call themselves) who lived on the lake full-time in a beautiful, hand-hewn log home.

There are more people of Finnish heritage in Minnesota than in any other state. I have always wondered why, but it turns out that, like other Scandinavian countries, improvements in overall health caused Finland's population to nearly triple during the 1800s. According to the book *They Chose Minnesota,* there was simply not enough farmland to support these additional people, making for poor economic conditions that were heightened by the famines in the 1860s. So, many came here to America in search of a better life. Personally, I think one of the best contributions the Finnish immigrants made to Minnesota culture was the sauna. Sweating in saunas is a longstanding winter tradition among cold-hardy Minnesotans. Our neighbors would fire up their sauna and let Mary Jo and I use it after they were done. Wow, was it great! If you really want to feel invigorated after a nice hot sauna session, run out and roll in the snow! I never could get Mary Jo to do it, but of course, I had to, just to show her I could.

Our neighbors had a fascinating dog named Timber, who was half-malamute and half-Chesapeake Bay retriever. He looked like a wolf but had the instincts of the Chessie. He loved the water, and he loved to retrieve. I will never forget tossing a rock about the size of a baseball into the lake (before it froze over) in about four feet or five feet of water for him to retrieve. He would dive down, and 90 percent of the time, he'd come up with the exact rock I threw! I was absolutely amazed. I started marking the rocks, so I knew it was the right one. The beach was rocky, so the rock I'd toss was never the only rock lying at the bottom of the lake. To this day, it is one of the most amazing feats I have ever seen by a dog. Or, maybe I am just easily amused.

Timber really liked us, and our sled dogs were fine with him being around, so he would often come over for a visit. I don't know if I ever saw him go into the neighbor's house; he seemed impervious to the cold. He would go into their garage or small shed, but he didn't seem to like the warm house. Another amusing thing he did, which I really appreciated, was bring us frozen walleye. Lake Vermillion, in the winter, is a popular ice fishing destination. Fishermen would cut several holes in the ice and set little tip-ups so when a fish strikes, the tip with a flag on it pops up, and you run to that hole to hopefully pull in the fish. When a fish is caught, fishermen lay it on the ice, and it freezes solid. Then, when they are done for the day, they collect any fish they happen to catch and head home. Well, the lake was Timber's stomping ground, especially in the winter as he traveled all over the ice. He could be an intimidating-looking dog if you didn't know him. We figured that while he was out on his rounds, he would come across a frozen walleye on the ice and decide to grab it and bring it home. I am not sure whether the fisherman didn't see him do it or they were afraid of him, but he brought us a fish probably every week. At first, we didn't know what to do with it as it wasn't our fish, so we would make Timber drop it and then leave it at the end of our dock in case some fisherman followed Timber's tracks back to our cabin looking for their fish. At the end of the day, when it got dark, and all the fishermen were gone from the lake if the fish was still there, we figured it was ours, and it became an amazing dinner. To this day, walleye is one of our favorite fish dinners. For the entire winter, no fisherman ever claimed a fish off our dock. Of course, maybe they saw Timber lying up in the yard, keeping an eye on that fish. Today, Timber would have a hard time finding any fish as the sport has evolved, and ice fishermen don't sit out on the ice anymore. They have heated structures. Some have even become castles that are towed behind a truck, and you drive them out on the ice where you have all the comforts of home.

That winter, we bought an old yellow skidoo snowmobile for $100 to groom our trails on the lake. This was an old machine with a pull-cord start because this was before electric starters were even around. We named our machine "Old Yeller," and she was a cantankerous old thing. Some days, she would start on the first yank of the pull cord, and other days, you could pull on that cord until it felt like your arm was going to fall off before she would start. Occasionally, she simply wouldn't start at all. We never figured out how to get her started on a regular basis. I guess it was just another case situation where I got what I paid for.

Lake trails are great because they tend to stay smooth, and you don't have to worry about tree branches hitting you in the face as you are cruising down the trail. The downside of any lake trail is that it tends to drift in with snow when there is any kind of wind. We really had a nice trail groomed, one that followed the shoreline down the lake for about five miles. The trail looped around a small island and then headed home, so it was basically an out-and-back trail, with the turnaround being the island. So, each time we took the snowmobile out, we essentially groomed the trail twice: once on the way out and once on the way home.

Our training schedule was pretty steady that winter, almost to the point of being obsessive. I suppose that's my nature. When I commit to something, I am all in. Of course, on occasion, that can backfire. The holidays came around, and on New Year's Day, I wanted to train the dogs, but Mary Jo disagreed.

"It is a holiday," she said. "I think we should just have a rest day."

"We did," I countered. "We took Christmas off!"

She finally agreed we should train a team, so we ventured out despite it being a cold and very windy holiday.

I rushed out to groom the trail, wanting to get done with dog chores before my alma mater, Ohio State University, took the field in the Rose Bowl. I fired up Old Yeller and started down the trail, pulling the small groomer we made. Everything was going great until I got to the far end of the trail and started around the island; then Old Yeller started coughing and lurching. She finally quit altogether on the back side of the island. I tried to restart her—nothing! I started to run through options of what could have gone wrong to make her stop in the middle of the run. My heart sank as I opened the gas cap: sure enough, I had run out of gas! (Those old machines didn't have a gas gauge.) In my rush to get going, I failed to do the simplest pre-grooming check: Make sure you have enough gas!

Now, I had to walk five miles back to the cabin with my tail between my legs in the cold and wind. Trust me, I was so hot under the collar I didn't even feel cold on that long walk. When I finally got back to the cabin, Mary Jo was certainly concerned as I had been gone for so long. She hadn't been keen on training that day anyway, and I hated the idea of having to ask for her help in retrieving our snow machine. I decided against asking for her help, but I couldn't leave Old Yeller out on the lake. So it was going to be another long, cold five-mile walk with the gas can. I felt it was just punishment, and I didn't want to bring Mary Jo into it. But being the sweetheart that she is, she insisted on helping me out. We hooked up the dog team, and Mary Jo sat in the basket of the sled, holding a five-gallon metal gas can between her knees. She was not very comfortable, for sure.

The trip out to rescue Old Yeller took a while as the dogs were pulling two of us, plus five gallons of gas. We started around the island to where the machine had stalled, and then I dropped the snow hook through the ski tip on the machine to hold the dogs in place while I filled the gas tank. Finally, I got Old Yeller running. Mary Jo got on the sled and drove the dog team back to the cabin as I drove the snowmobile home. Mary Jo was never a fan of driving any of the snow machines we had over the years. I wonder if all the trouble we had with Old Yeller simply left her forever soured on snowmobiles. I will agree with her on one thing: dog teams are much more dependable. You never have to worry about a dog team not starting!

CHAPTER 11

Making a Go of It in Minnesota

Staying that winter in the cabin on the lake made us realize how much we liked Minnesota. We decided we wanted to live there until we figured out what we wanted to do with our lives. We had made some good friends with other sled dog people. One who we became closest to was Miles Johnson, a quirky Vietnam veteran who was great with dogs but had little interest in racing. I remember one time, while riding in his truck, I asked him why he didn't use his turn signals. He simply replied, "It is nobody's business which way I am going!" Another time, he proclaimed he had finally figured out how to make a small fortune running sled dogs! I asked him, "How?" He said, "Start with a large one!"

The upper Midwest had probably the nicest and most complete sled dog racing circuit in the lower forty-eight at the time. We started looking for a place to rent that was winterized, had running water, and had enough space to keep our sled dogs. Miles helped us find a two-hundred-acre farm near Cook with an old single-wide house trailer, a garage, and a small, run-down barn. The barn was in such rough shape that after every windstorm, I would look to see if it was still standing. But we had heat, running water, space for our dogs, and enough cleared land to put in a training trail. It was great! The farm was also only about half a mile from a National Forest Service road that was not plowed in the winter. It was a perfect dog trail that the state groomed for snowmobiles.

Another interesting aspect of the area was it was home to a pack of wolves. A pack may cover territory of fifty square miles, so I doubt this pack was living in our backyard, but we did see wolves a few times while we lived there. Minnesota is home to the largest population of wolves outside of Alaska. Wolf sightings are rare, but when you see one, you will certainly remember it. I saw a lone wolf two different times while hiking in the forests northeast of Cook. I have no doubt I saw him or her only because they allowed me to see them. Both times, I was mesmerized by their stare. They looked me straight in the eyes like they were staring straight into my soul. I had never before, and have never since, had a wild animal stare straight into my eyes like that. It literally made the hair stand up on the back of my neck. Yet, for some reason, I did not feel I was in danger. I didn't feel like they were about to attack me or anything. I love spending time outdoors, and I can honestly say that my interaction with those wolves was mesmerizing. It ranks up there with seeing the northern lights dancing in the Alaskan sky or an encounter I had with a bald eagle years later.

We also had encounters with wolves at our training site. We often trained the team on the forest service road and would park our dog truck on the gravel road that intersected it. We would turn our dogs loose before a training run, and of course, being dogs, they would urinate and mark everything around the trailhead. Well, if the wolf pack happened to cross the trail area where our dogs had been during the day, they would just tear it up, pawing and digging. Then, of course, they, too, would mark the area, peeing on everything in sight. The next day, if we came back to train there, it looked like a road grader had come through. Boy, was there a strong smell of urine!

We only crossed paths one time with the wolf pack during a training run. We were on a beautiful trail that began in a dense spruce forest and opened into a large stand of birch trees. At the far end, we crossed a small stream that fed a big beaver pond off to the right, with at least one active beaver house on it. (The funny thing is, I trained on this trail for years before noticing the beaver house. It took a friend of mine pointing it out for me to notice!) Another couple of miles down, the trail took a sweeping curve to the left, back into the pines, and then the turnaround in an open meadow would feed you back onto the trail heading home.

It was a beautiful run that day, sunny with temperatures about 20°F: perfect sled dog weather. The dogs were cruising down the trail, and they were happy, as was I. Mary Jo was waiting for us back at the truck. As we were heading back, rounding one last turn to approach the straightaway, I saw the wolf pack crossing the trail about halfway between me and the truck. Mary Jo saw them too and started running down the trail towards us. It truly was an amazing experience; those wolves never even acknowledged us, just crossed the trail and continued into the forest. The sight of those wolves really changed the demeanor of the dog team. They slowed down when they picked up the smell of the wolves.

The most amazing thing about seeing the pack that day was the huge black wolf that was head and shoulders bigger than the rest of the pack. It was unbelievable! After we were all done and had the dogs put away, we walked back to where the wolves crossed the dog trail, and we saw a huge paw print in the snow, obviously from the big black wolf. We measured it: it was six inches *from side to side*! It made our sled dog paw prints look like pinheads. Looking back on it now, that wolf reminds me of a dire wolf, an extinct canine that was significantly larger than the wolves that roam our planet today. Dire wolves played a major role in the recent drama series *Game of Thrones*. On the drive back to the farm, we were both pretty excited, talking about seeing these wolves. When I asked Mary Jo what she thought she was doing running towards the wolves, she said she was worried the wolves were going to attack the dogs, and she was going to try and help if they did. *Wow*, I thought, *that is one brave woman, most people would have run the other way*!

Years later, we had a few lone wolf encounters while spending our winters in Alaska. When out on a training run, I could tell we might be seeing a wolf long before they came into sight just by the dogs' behavior. They could smell them way before we would see them, but why would they be afraid of them? My two lead dogs at the time, Vinnie and Veto—brothers who were born in Bucks County, Pennsylvania— seemed to be afraid of them the first time they encountered them, even though there hadn't been a wolf in Pennsylvania since the early 1900s. This convinced me the dogs' reaction was instinctual, not learned. On three different occasions over the years, I remember going down the trail, coming around a curve, and seeing a lone wolf trotting down the trail maybe fifty yards ahead. The wolf would start running faster and pull away; then, we would start catching up. The wolf would trot down the trail, see us, and take off again. The dogs would slow down, clearly because they were nervous. This would happen a few times over a couple of miles. The wolf never left the trail; it just stayed comfortably ahead of us, almost playing a game of hide and seek. The first time it happened, my mind started playing tricks on me. It almost felt like we were being baited into following this single wolf into a trap, where we would come around a bend into the whole pack of wolves and be attacked! I laughed at myself and thought, *Get a grip.* A wolf attack is very rare, especially in an area as vast as the Alaskan wilderness.

The farm where Mary Jo and I lived in Minnesota had lots of wildlife living on the property—especially whitetail deer. Often out in the fields, we would see a herd that could be as many as a dozen deer. Over time, we noticed they were getting bolder and bolder, not seeming to be afraid of the dogs. Sometimes, while out training on the trails on the property, we would almost run into them before they would jump out of our way. Over time, deer began bedding down right next to the dog yard, and the dogs got so used to them they wouldn't even bark at them anymore. But if any other animal was around, coyote, bear, or wolf, the dogs would go crazy. I started to believe these deer were using the dogs like a security system. If the dogs were quiet, it was safe; if they started to bark, something might be up. After living with dogs for so many years, we could tell by the tone of their bark what they were barking about. If a dog was loose, you could tell by the intensity and excitement of its bark. If a person came down the driveway, their bark was a deeper, more serious bark—certainly a different tone. You almost felt like they were saying, *I am not sure what this is about, but I don't think you are supposed to be here.* Before they got used to the deer, we identified their "deer bark," an excited bark but certainly a less serious tone, as if they were saying, *what are you doing in our yard?*

The few years we lived in northern Minnesota were very special. As one who grew up in the outdoors and has a real appreciation for Mother Nature, I loved the wildlife we saw there. From bald eagles, to moose, to black bears, to timber wolves, and even a bobcat—they were all amazing creatures. And yet, the animal that caused me the most trouble while we lived there was a young skunk.

One cold fall night before we had any snow, with the temperature hovering around 20°F, the dogs started whooping and hollering outside. I could tell by their bark something was going on, so I got out of bed and turned on the outside lights. It looked like two dogs had some sort of rag they were tossing around and fighting over. I threw on a pair of coveralls and some boots, put my headlamp on, and went outside to see what was going on. When I got closer, I could see they were squabbling over a young, dead skunk. I called the dogs off, grabbed a shovel by the fence, and went to scoop it up. . . only to find that it wasn't dead! The skunk spun around and sprayed me right in the face. My eyes were on fire, I was having a hard time breathing, and I thought I was going to throw up.

"I have been sprayed by a skunk!" I yelled as I raced back into the house.

Mary Jo replied, "I know! Get out!"

I had to go back outside in the cold, strip down to my underwear, and get out of those stinky clothes while trying not to freeze to death. I came back into the house and started scrubbing my body with hydrogen peroxide and tomato juice to get rid of the smell. As you might imagine, I spent the night on the couch. Skunk spray has been compared to tear gas, and rightly so, as both are lachrymators, which are chemical substances designed to irritate the eyes and nose, causing redness, mucus production, and tears. I was eventually able to extract the skunk from the dog yard and hoped that in the morning, he would be gone. Sadly, the next morning, I went out, and the poor skunk was dead. Then, we started to wonder if the skunk had been rabid or not. Should we have it tested? Of course, the dogs were all vaccinated, but I wasn't. I called the state Department of Natural Resources, and they told me that if a human was in contact with the skunk in question, they would test it for free. If there was no human contact, and the dogs were vaccinated, there would be a $125 charge.

"I will say I was in contact with the skunk and save us the money," I told Mary Jo.

"That would be fine unless the skunk tests positive, and they require you to come in to get rabies shots," she pointed out. At the time, this consisted of a series of seventeen painful injections into the stomach muscles. All of a sudden, the $125 didn't seem that bad!

The current treatment has certainly changed: now you get one injection the day of exposure, then follow-ups on days three, seven, and fourteen with no stomachs involved. I was happy to learn the skunk was negative for rabies.

CHAPTER 12

❖

Finding a Job

One of the biggest difficulties we had living in Minnesota early on was my success in finding a job. There were jobs available, and even some good ones, but every time I applied for a position and got an interview, they would simply say I was too overqualified for the job, and they feared I wouldn't stay in the position. Mary Jo and I had moved to Minnesota thinking that spending a couple of winters with our dogs and clearing our heads would provide us time to think of what the next chapters of our lives would be. No doubt we would eventually make our way back to nutrition and science as we had invested so much of our lives in it, but a little time to do something different was exciting! Not being able to find a job was frustrating our goal of trying something new. However, my brother-in-law came through again. He was an executive at the time at one of the biggest taconite mines in the Iron Range. The mine had a large construction company doing work for them, re-bricking and pouring new refractory material into their kilns, where the taconite pellets were finalized. He knew the foreman and asked if they needed any help. The foreman said he could use another laborer and ultimately gave me the job.

The job didn't go so well in the beginning. In fact, for the first month, no one on the crew I was working with even acknowledged my presence. Can you imagine going to work every day and having your coworkers act like you don't exist? It was strange, but I needed the job, so I put up with it. When they did talk to me, they spoke down to me. Once, they told me to go to the tool crib and get them a "2 x 4 extender." I had no idea what that was, and it turned out there was a good reason I hadn't heard of this tool before—there is no such thing! I am sure they all got a good laugh out of my ignorance. You see, even before I started working there, I had three strikes against me in the minds of the guys in the crew. First, I wasn't from the Iron Range, so I wasn't local—I was an outsider. Second, it was no secret that I got my job because my brother-in-law was an executive, and of course, they thought I didn't earn my position. It didn't matter that they were short on laborers and needed bodies. But third, and probably the biggest strike against me, was that I was a college graduate. These were hard-working, blue-collar men, and they weren't big on advanced degrees. The only one on the crew who would talk to me was the foreman, who really had no choice, seeing as he was the boss. He tried to give me direction, but he wasn't always around. I just had to watch what the other guys did and follow their lead. I would eat lunch each day by myself and take my breaks by myself. It was tough work for sure; most of my time was spent running a ninety-pound jackhammer. But it paid well, and boy, did I get in shape. Most importantly, it allowed me time to work with our dogs.

After about a month, the crew started to soften their stance towards me. One thing I made sure they couldn't deny was that I was a good worker. I took on all the shit jobs and never complained. Finally, one of the oldest guys on the crew at least started to acknowledge me. When he finally did talk to me, what he said was quite surprising. We got paid weekly, and everyone on the crew threw in a few dollars to play paycheck poker. That is where you take the cents listed in the amount from your paycheck, plus the last three digits of the check number, and try to make the best poker hand: zeros are aces, and every other digit is face value. Whoever had the best hand won the pot, and then everyone went to the local bar, where the winner bought the first round. This old guy warned me never to win paycheck poker because I would have to go to the bar, and a few of these guys really wanted to get me away from work so they could beat the hell out of me. I had figured some didn't like me, but I really didn't think they would take it to that extreme. These guys were a little rough around the edges, and more than a few times, I heard stories about weekend bar fights, guys cashing their checks, heading to the bar, and coming home wasted and broke. One guy was out for a couple of months after he broke his leg in a bar fight. Most of them had weekend hunting camps or fishing cabins to get away on the weekends or during hunting season. They seemed to enjoy coming in on Monday morning to see who could tell the craziest weekend story. I don't know how any of them stayed married. Seemed like most of them were already on wife number two. Hearing some of their stories was pretty funny, but I knew better than to laugh at them.

One of the best stories I heard was about one of these guys' trips. One guy came in one Monday looking pretty rough, really hungover—no doubt he spent the weekend drinking and carousing. He had told his wife he was going for a weekend fishing trip. When he got home Sunday evening, he asked her why she hadn't packed him any underwear. She said she did. He couldn't find them; *where did she put them?* With an accusatory glare, she simply said, *in your fishing rod case.* He was busted! She figured he wasn't going fishing, and he proved her point by not ever taking his fishing rod out of the case. His day got even worse when he opened his lunch box that day back at work to see that the only thing she packed for his lunch was an empty whiskey bottle. It was really all I could do not to burst out laughing. They liked to say that hardly anyone from this laborers' union had lived past fifty years. I could believe it as these were macho tough guys who never wore respirators until they were required by law, even though sometimes these kilns were so dusty you could hardly see the guy working eight feet from you. Remember, this was long enough ago that the United States was just starting to regulate asbestos use.

A couple of months after I was hired, they brought in another laborer, a local just back from living in southern California. The story was that he was a member of the Mongols, a bad-ass outlaw motorcycle gang, and he got into some trouble and needed to get out of town. He sure looked the part—lots of tattoos and a look that said, "Don't mess with me." They called him Butch, but I have no idea what his real name was. Surprisingly, some of the crew seemed a bit intimidated by him. Maybe they knew more about him than I ever would, but for some reason, he took a liking to me—maybe because he wasn't one to follow the lead of everyone else. If the crew was going to ignore me, he was going to befriend me. One day, he gave me some real street credibility with the crew, which could have easily gone the wrong way. I was standing on some scaffolding, wearing the required safety harness with a safety line attached to the railings on the scaffolding in case I fell. The idea was that the safety line would stop you from crashing to the ground. My safety line was dangling down, and Butch jumped up and grabbed onto my safety line and swung from it. His weight almost pulled me off the scaffolding. He was just goofing around, laughing, so I turned around and swung my foot towards him to get him to let it go, joking as well. Well, there were two problems with this maneuver: first, I wore steel-toed boots, and second, his weight on the rope lurched me forward unexpectedly. I kicked him right in the mouth and split his lip wide open! Blood started pouring out, and all the guys in the crew just froze and watched in amazement, wide-eyed and mouths agape. They couldn't believe Joe College had the balls enough to kick this tough-guy Mongol in the mouth! Honestly, I was a bit surprised as well; I certainly didn't mean to touch him. My next thought was, *Holy shit, what did I just do!* I was relieved when he continued to laugh since he'd started the whole episode and seemed fine with how I reacted. He just kept wiping the blood away. I have no doubt it wasn't the worst thing that ever happened to him. Working in that construction crew for a couple of years was a pretty amazing experience. Although my coworkers completely ignored me for the first few weeks, when I finally left, they had a cake for me! I had really won them over by simply working hard and just being me.

CHAPTER 13

◆

Jessie, Jack, and Hannibal Join the Team

My graduate work in nutrition and the ways it affects stamina and exercise in running dogs was published and well-received, which opened numerous doors for me. Many people wanted to hear me speak, and this exposure allowed me to meet and become friends with some of the top sled dog racers and bird dog trainers in the world. This, of course, also gave us access to some really good dogs. Having Dr. Kronfeld as a friend and a mentor opened doors for us as well. One of the best lead dogs, who came to me out of the blue, was only supposed to be with me for one season. Dr. Kronfeld remained in contact with a former veterinary student who had moved to Alaska to practice veterinary medicine and became a top sprint sled dog racer. She was taking a year off from racing to have a baby and was looking for a temporary home for two of her best dogs—a pair of brothers named Jessie and Jack. Dr. Kronfeld recommended Mary Jo and I as temporary caretakers. The dogs flew from Fairbanks to Philadelphia, where I picked them up. Jessie wasn't quite so sure about me. It was obvious he had quite a bond with his owner, and he wasn't so sure about this journey. Of course, I chalked up his indifference to jet lag as they had just flown 4,300 miles with three stops. Jack, on the other hand, was happy to see anyone he met. Just like kids, these dogs are all different. Here are two brothers, raised side-by-side their entire lives with completely different personalities. I will say, initially, they weren't too crazy about the heat and humidity on the East Coast, but we certainly had a lot fewer mosquitoes than the interior of Alaska! They soon adapted to their new environment.

For me, it was love at first sight. Jessie looked like quite an athlete, with long flowing lines and rippling muscles. He was a big, deep-chested grey and white male with beautiful, deep blue eyes. He was an alpha male for sure and an amazing lead dog. He would only run in lead. Running lead in a dog team can be a lot of pressure, so most good race leaders enjoy a day or two off from running lead. Not Jessie! If he wasn't in lead, he was not happy. He would simply sulk and act uninterested in running at all! Jack was the complete opposite. He was just a happy-go-lucky dog who got along with everybody. He just liked to run; he had no interest in running lead. He had a dark, dirty grey coat with longer hair and brown eyes. He was more slab-sided than his brother. He had one annoying habit that we eventually found humorous; you simply could not keep him on a leash when we went training. We had a truck with compartments for each dog to transport them to the training site. Then, when we arrived, we would let the dogs out of the truck and put them on short leashes attached to eye bolts that were around the bottom of the truck. From there, we would put them in harnesses and hook them into the team to go on our run. Each time I let Jack out and put him on his leash on the side of the truck, I walked around to the other side of the truck to find Jack was already there! He was jumping on me, barking, like, "Let's go!" The first couple of times it happened, I thought I just didn't put the leash on properly, then I thought it was the result of a bad snap. I tried different snap designs, but Jack could escape from any snap I could come up with. I have never before or since had a dog who could break away from a snap any quicker than Jack. I finally appreciated what an escape artist he had become and just didn't worry about putting him on a leash. He would run around the truck loose, barking and acting as a cheerleader, getting the others fired up. I never worried he would run off because he just wanted to be by my side, and he wanted to run in the team. I only had to worry when we had a female in season because he was a young male, and hormones superseded even his desire to be a sled dog!

On the other hand, Jessie was as serious and focused a dog we have ever had. Over time, Jessie really became my dog in every way. We connected on a special level. He was flawless on his commands; we could be going down the trail at full speed, and on command, I could move him a little to the right or a little to the left. He would take a full ninety-degree turn in either direction on a simple one-word command. I have had a lot of amazing dogs in my life, but the connection I had with Jessie was very rare.

Mary Jo with Jessie and Pitch in lead at the
starting chute in Saranac Lake, NY
Photo credit: Fil Fina III

The difficult part was we only had Jessie and Jack for one season. I knew they were going back to Alaska, where they were born and where they were a big part of one of the top sprint teams in Alaska.

I tried not to think about it and just focus on the moment. I knew the deal going in. What I didn't think about was how much I would become attached to them. Jack for his goofiness, and Jessie for the connection we had developed in such a short time. I offered to buy them both from their owners—Dr. Kronfeld even went to bat for us. Eventually, she let us buy Jack, but Jessie was just too great a lead dog for her to give up. So, with unbelievable sadness, we sent him back to Alaska. It was one of the hardest things I had ever done.

Later that year, something amazing occurred. We got a call from Jessie's owner in Alaska, and she said she couldn't believe it, but Jessie was no longer her dog. Jessie was born in her yard, and she raised and trained him. He had led her team for three years, and they won many races together. . . but she realized that Jessie had become my dog. She told me that when she started training him that fall, he would not do anything she told him. In fact, he often did the opposite: if she asked him to turn right, he would turn left and vice versa. She just couldn't believe it. She said she simply wanted him to be happy, and she realized that would only come when he was with me. That was an incredible gesture for her to send him back to us. It speaks to the kind of person she was. We were so happy to get Jessie back, and boy, was he excited when we picked him up at the airport!

I may have thought myself lucky to get Jessie back on our team, but I would soon see just *how* lucky I was to have him. At the construction job site, the kilns we were working in were about 128 feet long and 30 feet high. They were lined with bricks and had refractory material covering the final thirty inches at each end. Refractory materials are resistant to high temperatures and are used predominantly as furnace linings for the processing of elevated-temperature materials. This refractory material was poured like wet concrete over thick stainless steel plates with rebar sticking out about six inches to give the refractory something to grab onto. The poured refractory would provide a nice smooth surface for the ends of the kilns. The bricks lasted much longer than the refractory material. Over time, we had to jackhammer and haul out all the bricks and then replace them (we did the same with the refractory material, only more often). We used ninety-pound jackhammers to break the refractories, and after we got one section done, the kiln operators would come in and rotate the kiln upward, so we were only jackhammering in a downward position. These stainless-steel plates weighed ninety-two pounds and were held in place by two heavy bolts. During the day, we would jackhammer and clean a section to expose the steel plates under it, and that night, the mine workers would replace the steel plates we exposed and rotate the kiln so the next morning, we would have more refractory on the bottom to remove. For a week, my partner and I worked in the kiln first thing in the morning. Because I was the young guy, I would go in first and start jackhammering. The vibration was severe, and because any loose material at the top of the kiln came falling down, we were required to wear hard hats.

After a week, we had two more days of work to finish the job. That Saturday, on a cool, crisp Minnesota autumn morning, I went out on a training run with Jessie in lead. It was too early for snow, so we were still training on our heavy three-wheeled rig. We headed out our quarter-mile driveway, turned right, and proceeded down the dirt road. About two miles later, we came to an intersection, and then we would turn left and go another mile. Then, we came upon a small gravel pit on the left. We would turn onto a small lane that would lead us about a half-mile to the base of the gravel pit. We would start climbing up and loop around the top rim of the gravel pit to the back side, then back down, eventually arriving back at the base. Finally, we would head out to the road and turn to go home. The top of the rim was about a hundred feet above the road leading into it. It became a beautiful way to turn the dogs around and head home. We would just climb up the hundred feet to follow the rim around the top of the pit and back down the other side. Dogs are creatures of habit, so once they learn a trail, they always run it the same way. It becomes repetitive. Jessie had it down.

That morning, he did something I didn't expect. Halfway around the top of the rim, he turned ninety degrees to the right and jumped over the edge of the rim. We faced a hundred-foot drop at about a forty-five-degree slope! The rig I stood on was heavy, and if I let go of it and bailed on the team, the rig would start careening down the side of the gravel pit, no doubt running over the dogs. With no time to think, I flipped the rig on its side and started sliding down the side of the gravel pit, not letting go, trying to dig in my feet to slow down. I wasn't about to let the rig run over my dogs. The rig dragged me to the bottom of the pit, tearing up my knees and elbows on the way down. When we finally came to a stop, I had a hard time getting to my feet. My jeans were completely ripped and blood-stained. I had abrasions and a severe case of gravel rash. My left knee was swollen and excruciatingly painful—no doubt I hit a rock during my descent. I struggled to flip the rig back onto its wheels, where I was able to lock the brakes and untangle the dogs. It was a tough ride back to the kennel. I was pretty much standing on one leg, trying not to put any weight on my left leg as my knee swelled up like a balloon. But I couldn't wrap my head around what Jessie had just done. *Why would he just jump over the side of the gravel pit?* We had been around that trail dozens of times, and the dogs enjoyed it.

By Sunday, both my knees were swollen, especially the left one. It was difficult to walk, and I spent most of the weekend with ice packs on my knees. I was back at work on Monday morning, walking rather stiffly but ready to head back into the kiln to finish the job. My partner noticed the obvious discomfort I was in and said he would go into the kiln first. He hooked up the ninety-pound jackhammer, dragged it into the kiln, and started breaking loose the refractory. Within minutes, one of the ninety-two-pound pieces of steel dropped from the ceiling and hit him right on the head, crushing him! I raced to get help. It seemed like forever before an ambulance arrived to rush him to the hospital. It turned out that when the crew had replaced that stainless steel plate, they didn't completely tighten the bolts. The vibration from the jackhammer caused the nuts to come loose, and down it came. Luckily, he survived, but he had a tough life from that point on—he was permanently disabled. I felt horrible, as I was the first one in the kiln every day except that day, and it felt like that should have been me. To this day, I can't get it out of my head; I was the first one in the kiln every day for a week, and the only reason I wasn't there first on Monday is because Jessie took the team over the side of a gravel pit and I got injured! Why did Jesse do that? He had never done it before, and he never did it again. The only thing that stopped me from being the one crushed under that heavy piece of steel was Jessie behaving totally out of character! Was it fate or divine intervention with the good Lord looking after me?

Another memorable dog came to us from a small village in Alaska. Hannibal was a long-bodied and deep-chested black dog with a white stripe down his face and piercing blue eyes. He was an incredibly strong, hard-driving dog. He really put pressure on the lead dogs to go faster. There was no letup in Hannibal as he drove as hard as he could for as long as he could.

There are various positions in a dog team: lead dogs are obviously the most important as they are your steering wheel. With no reins, you need to have a strong connection with your lead dog to rely on voice commands. Think about having eight to sixteen dogs in a team in front of you as you are standing on a sixteen-pound sled traveling over twenty miles per hour, and the only control you have to turn right or left is a single command to the leaders. The two dogs behind your leaders are called *point* or *swing dogs*. They are the ones who really set the pace and keep up the speed. Behind the point dogs, all the pairs are *team dogs* until you get to the two dogs just in front of the sled, which are called *wheel dogs*. Wheel dogs must be agile and athletic enough to get the sled around corners.

Hannibal was a wonderful point dog, but he was not perfect by any means. He had his quirks, as I guess we all do. There is no doubt he had a tough life in Alaska before coming to us. He would try to attack anyone wearing a red plaid wool coat, a style that was quite popular back in those days. We found this out one day when a friend of ours, who Hannibal had always been very friendly towards, came over wearing a red, plaid wool coat for the first time. Hannibal lunged at him! Dogs are supposed to be color blind, but obviously, Hannibal could distinguish the pattern even if he couldn't tell the color. It took us a while to figure out what was happening. We just couldn't believe a color or a pattern would trigger his aggression. I can't help but think someone wearing that style jacket must have abused him, and he never forgot it.

Hannibal was also very protective of the dog truck when he was in it. The truck we would transport the dogs in was a heavy-duty one-ton truck with dual rear wheels and a customized dog box built on the frame. There were individual insulated compartments for the dogs with doors that had stainless steel expanded metal grates for warmer weather and clear Plexiglas louvered covers for cold weather travel. The dogs could see out the doors to enjoy the scenery as we crisscrossed the United States and Canada. Hannibal was fine in his compartment until a stranger came up to his door and tried to look at him. He would launch himself at the door, snarling, growling, and attacking the door—intimidating anyone who had the bad misfortune of trying to peer in.

Our dogs always traveled in comfort

We learned to use this behavior to our advantage. Every year, we would travel to Canada to race, often to lovely towns such as Kirkland, Quebec; Winnipeg, Manitoba; and Minden and North Bay, Ontario. For twenty winters, we also traveled all the way across Canada and raced in wonderful places like Fort St. John and Fort Nelson, British Columbia, and then on to Watson Lake and Whitehorse, Yukon, on our way to Alaska. When you cross into Canada, you must go through Canadian customs, also known as Canada Border Services Agency (CBSA). It seemed every border crossing was different every year. Some years, they would just ask us a few questions, look at the health certificates for the dogs, and wave us through. On a couple of occasions, after looking at our paperwork, they told me to pull over to a parking lot, asked me to get out of the truck, and emptied the entire cab to look at everything. Then, they simply set everything down next to your truck on the pavement. It didn't matter if it was snowing, blowing, or raining. When they gave you the "okay," you had to repack your truck. I realize they were just doing their job, but it was an ordeal. Occasionally, we got an agent who was either in a bad mood or bored or maybe new to the job and just wanted to be thorough, but he would ask to see each dog. We certainly weren't trying to hide anything, but having an agent inspect each dog was very time-consuming.

We had crossed the border enough times to have experienced this extended inspection more than once, and when we got Hannibal and saw how protective he was of the truck, we knew exactly where to put him. We placed Hannibal in the first compartment by the driver's side door, as the border agents would inevitably start at the front of the truck on the driver's side and work their way around the truck. When the agent looked in at him, Hannibal would go nuts and launch himself at the door. The agent would get scared, then step back and say, "They look good," and wave us through. It sure saved us a lot of time at the border. If we had to take every dog out for them to see, we lost at least an hour. When your trip is 4,200 miles long, every hour is important.

Honestly, I never felt bad about it as we weren't doing anything illegal or trying to smuggle anything into Canada, although I did know another musher who used his dogs to provide the cover, literally, for some illegal smuggling. He was a bit of a pothead and was trying to figure out how to get his marijuana, for personal use only, to Alaska while going through Canada. Remember, this was years ago when it was illegal *everywhere*. When you travel with that many dogs, obviously, they will generate waste (poop), and you just don't leave it lying where they deposit it. So, we each had a poop bucket lined with a disposable plastic liner, and you would carry a small shovel and a rake to clean up the poop and deposit it in the bucket. Usually, once a day, you would dispose of the bag with the poop in it and start with a clean bag the next day. Well, this musher would double-bag his marijuana and put it at the bottom of the bucket under the poop bag. He wouldn't change the poop bag before he got to the border crossing going into Canada. At the crossing, if the border guard started going through his truck, if he took the lid off the poop bucket and looked inside and saw what was in it, he would immediately snap the lid back on and move on to looking at something else. They never looked under the poop bag!

I did have one interesting interaction with a border guard. He was not a Canadian guard but a U.S. Border Patrol Agent, who I encountered as I was trying to get into Alaska from Canada—in other words, back into my own country. I pulled up to the gate, and he came out and asked me a few questions: where I was from, where I was going, how long I was going to be in Alaska, etcetera. Then he looked at my paperwork and said, "Pull over there and come into the building. I have a few more questions for you." He had a rather suspicious look on his face, and as I parked my truck, I thought, *This makes me nervous.* So, I went inside, and he started asking me the same questions.

"You don't sound like you are from Pennsylvania," he commented.

"Well, I didn't grow up there; I grew up in the Midwest, in Ohio," I replied.

"You don't sound like you're from there either. You sound like you are Canadian," he said.

"I did live a few years in northern Minnesota," I explained, "and people have said I do sound like I am from Canada."

"I don't think you are American at all!" He said, to my shock. "I think you are one of those damn French Canadians who want to live here in Alaska with your dogs!"

I honestly started looking around to see if there was a camera, and this was a *Candid Camera* moment. "I don't know what you want me to say," I said. "You have my driver's license; you see my paperwork."

"Where did you live in northern Minnesota?"

"Cook," I said.

He thought for a minute and said, "That's interesting; I used to be a cop in that area. What was that little town northeast of Cook? It began with a B—was it Brainard?"

Wow, I thought, *he is trying to trap me!* He obviously used to live up there. I said, "No, Brainard is down by the Twin Cities. You must mean Buyck."

Right then, he knew I was telling the truth, as Buyck is this lovely little town on the edge of Kabetogama State Forest, with the Vermillion River running through it. There were probably not more than five hundred people living there at the time. If I knew the name and location of Buyck, as we had friends who lived there, I obviously was familiar with the area. He begrudgingly wished me a good day and sent me on my way.

Hannibal earned the nickname "Hannibal the Cannibal" as he was also a bit of a fighter. If another male dog looked at him the wrong way, Hannibal might go after him—behavior we called being "Hannibalized." So we always had to be watching him, especially when we had them all loose. When you have twenty-five dogs running around together, there is always potential for trouble. Dogs are pack animals, and they establish a pecking order. It is better to be towards the top of the pecking order rather than the bottom!

Hannibal's aggression is a great example of the difficulty of our early years in sled dog ownership. As I mentioned, I originally started out with rescue sled dogs—dogs that needed a new home. There is usually a reason they are looking for a new home, whether they have some sort of behavior issue or something that made them available. We see that every day with shelter dogs, there is usually a reason they are in shelters. Some of the reasons dogs end up in shelters are just ridiculous: I recently heard a woman dropped off a lovely young cocker spaniel at the shelter because they got a new carpet, and the dog no longer matched the carpet! Some people just shouldn't own dogs. However, some dogs have true behavioral struggles.

Even years later, when we would buy an occasional dog, it would often become obvious why that dog was available for purchase. Hannibal was a perfect example. He was an amazing sled dog, but he certainly had his issues and could be tough to handle. I have always believed there are no bad dogs, just bad owners who have created a difficult situation for the dog. Dogs live in the moment, and if you remove them from a difficult situation, they often bounce back. We have seen that in so many dogs over the years, including Hannibal the Cannibal.

PART 3

GROWING OUR FUTURE AND OUR FAMILY

CHAPTER 14

How Annamaet Started

After a couple of years of living the dream in Minnesota with our dogs, Mary Jo and I realized it was time to get back and make good use of our studies and all the work we had done in nutrition and exercise in dogs. We moved back to Pennsylvania with all the dogs and started to plan our future. While we were laying the groundwork to begin Annamaet Petfoods, a longtime friend, Rick, offered me a job working for their family construction company to help us get by. As I have mentioned, I had consulted for some pet food companies, and it didn't work out, as they were more concerned with the bottom line than good nutrition. I really became disenchanted with the whole pet food industry. Over the years, my friends kept telling us to start our own pet food company. Our research taught us what you need to do to make a great pet food. I was confident in what I had learned to formulate great diets for my dogs. That is how we got into the pet food industry.

The pet industry has really changed during the years I raised dogs. It wasn't that many years ago that 90 percent of pet owners in the U.S. couldn't tell the difference between the best pet food and the worst pet food because they didn't worry about coat, stool quality, or life expectancy. One thing we learned in the Great Recession of 2008 is that the pet industry is recession-proof. Many pet parents consider their dogs and cats to be an essential part of the family, like children. This phenomenon has become known as the humanization of pets, and currently, in the United States, 95 percent of dog and cat owners now fall into the category of pet owners who see their pets as family members. This is a trend that is growing worldwide. Millennials are a big part of this, as many are forgoing having children and are having fur babies instead.

Mary Jo and I created Annamaet Petfoods in 1986, starting with two formulas. That number has increased significantly, and we've moved into treats, supplements, and cat foods. We now ship our products all around the world. The mission of Annamaet is to provide optimum nutrition to maximize the health and well-being of dogs and cats worldwide while maintaining a responsibility to the environment and our natural resources. With our background in science and nutrition, we were confident we could make a better product by using superior ingredients with higher levels of quality vitamins and minerals from non-tainted sources. We could also maximize longevity while maintaining a great quality of life. We started doing feeding trials (initially with our dog, Salt!) as soon as the company began and continued those for more than thirty years on eight generations of dogs. American Association of Feed Control Officials (AAFCO, an independent organization that has been charged by local, state, or federal laws to regulate the sale and distribution of pet foods) requires feeding trials of eight dogs and four blood tests. On Annamaet's two most recent products, we did feeding trials on more than eighty dogs and measured thirty-six blood parameters. When we release a formula, we are confident in the safety and efficacy of the product.

One thing I quickly learned about the pet industry is that every ingredient you see on the side panel of a bag, the back of a can, or the wrapper on a frozen block of raw comes in at least four different quality levels. Not all chicken or fish are created equal. This makes it impossible to evaluate a pet food by simply reading the label. This explains why you can see two products with almost identical ingredient lists on the shelf at the pet store, yet they have such a difference in price. Or if you feed them to your dogs or cats, you can see a big difference in how they are digested. The quality of ingredients and processing can vary tremendously from product to product.

Our graduate work showed that you could increase stamina in running dogs by altering levels of proteins, fats, and carbohydrates. Even with that research readily available, there wasn't a dry food I could trust to give us the results we were looking for. The dry foods available simply weren't good enough. So, early in our career, we fed our dogs a mixture of mostly raw meat and dry food that we balanced with vitamins and minerals. That was part of the push for us to start Annamaet. We were confident that we could put together a dry food that any canine athlete could consume and be successful while competing in any arena. For many years, some of the big commercial pet food companies were doing full sponsorships in Alaska of some of the top distance teams there. The teams would get free food for the year. Although the food was fine for the summers when dogs weren't doing much, during heavy training and in any big distance race, it simply didn't hold up. A couple of mushers told me that they would open a bag of their sponsored food and empty it, then fill it with Annamaet, reseal it, and ship it out to the checkpoints. They knew if they wanted to be competitive in the race, they needed to take their dogs' diet to the next level. One top musher told me if they had to buy food, Annamaet was the only product they would consider paying for. A lot of top show dogs were using Annamaet as well because owners loved the energy level and the glossy coat it provided. One dog that won the Best-in-Show at Westminster Kennel Club in NYC ate only Annamaet its entire life. Yet their kennel was sponsored by a big commercial dog food company, so they got all the accolades. Annamaet was never mentioned, and honestly, I am fine with that as I know the truth.

Because I make dry food, people will ask if I am anti-raw. I am not at all; in fact, I fed raw to my sled dogs before raw was niche. Even today, one of our most popular products, Annamaet Enhance, is a vitamin and mineral supplement to help balance homemade and raw diets. Raw has really grown in popularity as many people think the dog is an extension of a wolf and should be fed as such. We should, however, remember that a dog's lifespan is significantly longer than that of a wolf. Most wolves only eat every three to five days, and they must chase down and kill their prey. On the other hand, most dogs live in air conditioning in the summer and a heated building in the winter. They are not only fed daily but many dogs are fed multiple times a day. It is no wonder, then, that obesity is the number one health problem facing dogs and cats today.

A few people even believe that dogs can't break down carbohydrates. That is simply not true. Dogs were domesticated during the Paleolithic era, about fifteen- to thirty thousand years ago. They were domesticated by humans before any other plant or animal, including food crops and livestock like horses and cattle.

One of the ways we evolve genetically is by duplicating genes, and of course, the generational turnover in dogs is much quicker than in humans, so evolution happens much quicker as well. The amylase gene determines our ability to break down starches. Recently, a comprehensive study out of Sweden compared the DNA of wolves and various breeds of dogs. They found that wolves have two copies of the amylase gene, whereas dogs have between four and thirty copies, depending on the breed. Their results show the conversion of the early ancestors of the modern dog to prosper on a diet with increased levels of starch compared to carnivorous wolves. This was a crucial step in the early domestication of dogs.

The three macronutrients in any diet are protein, fat, and carbohydrates. Most raw diets minimize the level of carbohydrates, which, of course, increases the level of protein and fat. There are twice the number of calories in a gram of fat compared to a gram of protein or carbohydrate. This means higher fat levels really increase caloric density, thus calorie levels. So, pet owners who feed their pets a raw diet really need to be concerned about their pets becoming overweight. Studies have shown that obesity in dogs can shorten their lifespan by two years. Over half of the dogs in the United States are currently obese, and only 20 percent of their owners realize it. Experts estimate that more than 100 million dogs and cats in the United States are obese. Most dogs start to become overweight or obese when they are only two years old. One of my goals is to make pet parents aware of these concerns. Proper exercise and a good diet can optimize the longevity of our beloved pets.

With advances in the pet industry brought by technology and advances in science, pet foods, in general, are much better today compared to when we began Annamaet. There are many quality dry foods and raw formulas available today. I would caution pet parents if they choose to go the raw dog food route to be careful of the fat content. I was surprised to see the fat levels on some of the best-known brands to be higher than the fat levels we fed our sled dogs during the race season in Alaska, where they were burning lots of calories. My concern would be if you cut back their feed intake enough to keep them from getting overweight, will they then be getting enough vitamins and minerals to optimize longevity? Studies have shown that appropriate levels of vitamins and minerals in your dog's diet have been associated with increased longevity and a decrease in overall health issues. A major study just released has shown that daily multivitamin supplements will help memory and slow age-associated cognitive decline in humans.

I have no doubt that the higher levels of vitamins in Annamaet products are part of the reason we hear from happy customers that their pets, who have been fed Annamaet, live long and healthy lives.

Our commitment to nutrition and science has certainly been augmented by having a second nutritionist on staff. Dr. Joe Wakshlag is a board-certified veterinary nutritionist who is a dear friend. I have known Joe since his first year of veterinary school. He is Annamaet's staff nutritionist and the only person to drive with me to Alaska twice. I guess everyone else thought one 4,200-mile drive was enough! Looking back, we had some pretty good laughs on those trips. One year, we raced in the lower forty-eight before heading to Alaska, so we didn't start heading north until February. We were cruising across the prairies of Western Canada late into the night. There are limited hotel rooms available in some of those small prairie towns, and they fill up early. At one of our stops, Joe and I got the last room. It happened to be Valentine's Day, and we didn't get just any room—it was the honeymoon suite! We really had no choice but to take it. The hour was getting late, and the next hotel was another fifty miles down the road. Who knew if they would have any rooms or even be open? We were laughing and heading to the room; I said, "Wait until our wives hear about this." We started laughing even harder when we entered the room—there was only one bed, and it was heart-shaped! Then we noticed the mirror on the ceiling!

After thirty-seven years of successfully running Annamaet Petfoods, I will admit I am still more comfortable with the nutrition side than the business side. We have stayed loyal to our simple mission, with honesty and integrity at the core. When we started Annamaet in 1986, Salt, in her retirement years, became a major factor in launching Annamaet Petfoods. Why was Salt, out of all the many dogs we raced, so important in launching our company? Salt was the finickiest eater ever. At times, it seemed she didn't want to eat anything. It doesn't matter how great the nutritional value of a product is; if it isn't palatable and a dog doesn't want to eat it—game over! We figured if we could get Salt to eat and enjoy the food, every other dog would as well.

I didn't realize how long and arduous a task it would be to develop a nutritious formula that tasted good to Salt. During recipe development, you can't just produce *one* bag of food. The minimum batch at the time was 4000 lbs. During production, you discard some product at the beginning of the run, and you lose some at the end of the run because it doesn't meet the nutrient levels you are targeting. Our first batch was a complete failure as far as Salt was concerned, though the rest of our dogs thought the food was just fine, as did many of our friends' dogs, so thankfully, nothing went to waste. With the second batch, Salt seemed more interested, but we decided that still wasn't good enough, so we went back to the drawing board. The third batch was even better, and we felt we were on the right track. Finally, in the fourth batch, we nailed it: Salt loved it, and we were ecstatic! Our foods are still known today for being palatable, and I like to think this is Salt's influence—still resonating all these years later. We ended up going through four batches and sixteen thousand pounds of dog food before we got one she would eat! Luckily, the rest of our dogs weren't so finicky.

I would have to think that no dog in sled dog sports has ever had their final race in a team with as big and loud of an audience as Salt did. She was approaching her tenth birthday, and we knew it was probably time for her to retire from racing. This was years before good joint supplements like Annamaet Endure were developed to extend the careers of canine athletes. The Philadelphia Phillies, a Major League Baseball team, were playing the New York Mets at the old Veterans Stadium in 1979. The Phillies weren't having a very good season, and on July 5th, the *Philadelphia Inquirer* reported: *If the main attraction has not exactly been up to par, the Phillies are compensating in other ways. Tonight's pre-game is a "Winter Carnival" featuring iceless skating on an Eskimo's answer to Astroturf, Christmas music by the Greater Overbrook String Band (dressed in snowflake costumes), and a dogsled race between Richie Ashburn and Harry Kalas. Now, all we need is another miracle on Broad Street.*

I was asked to provide a team for the event. I knew we wanted to be a part of this unique celebration, and I knew who I wanted to lead our team. There would be two teams racing head-to-head, with two famed Philadelphia Phillies announcers, Harry Kalas and Richie Ashburn, on the back of each team.

The one dog I knew I could trust to handle the crowd of about thirty thousand people with all the noise and lack of defined trail would be Salt. The Phillies rolled out the red carpet for her when we arrived. They had us park our dog trucks under the stadium, and several of the players came by to see the dogs before the game. Honestly, I was more than a little nervous about the race itself. How were the dogs going to handle the crowd and the noise? Salt handled it beautifully. With her in lead, it was like driving a car. If I asked, she would move a little to the right or the left, which was important as we were racing around the *inside of a major league baseball field*.

I will never forget seeing all the players on the top step of the dugout, watching in amazement a sled dog race right in Philadelphia, in the middle of Veterans Stadium. The Philadelphia fans were boisterous, as Philadelphia fans are known to be (I can say that because I am married to one). I wonder if they had any idea that they would be going to a baseball game and a sled dog race would break out! It was a highlight for me as well. I was cruising around the inside of the stadium with Richie Ashburn by my side on the rig. For years, I had watched him broadcast Phillies games on TV. He was true Philadelphia royalty—a Phillies Hall of Fame player and now a color commentator. I thought, *whatever you do, don't let him fall off and get hurt.* Unfortunately, the other team didn't handle it as well—they had trouble navigating the stadium as there was no defined trail. Salt's last run was in front of thousands of screaming fans at Veterans Stadium—what a way to end a career!

CHAPTER 15

◆

Training in the New Jersey Pine Barrens

Back living in Pennsylvania, with the help of some friends, we found one of the best training areas in the Eastern United States: the New Jersey Pine Barrens, also known as the home of the Jersey Devil. The Pine Barrens is an amazing area covering 1.1 million acres of pine forests on sandy soil. Crisscrossed with roads, fire lanes, and trails, running in the Pine Barrens feels like running on a beach. The dogs love it as it is so soft—sometimes too soft, like running in soft snow. Interestingly, all of our dogs who were born and raised in Alaska would, after their first run in this soft sand in N.J., reach down and take a bite of sand, which, of course, they would quickly start spitting back out! Why would they do that, you ask? In Alaska, after a training run or when you stop for a rest on snow, they reach down and take a big bite of snow to cool off. Dogs are creatures of habit, so when they got to the Pine Barrens and ran in that soft sand, it felt so close to their runs on soft snow that without thinking, they just grabbed a bite. Trust me, it usually only happened once! By the time we discovered the Pine Barrens, we had also started to train off the front of an ATV, as the dogs could easily pull it through the soft sand.

I was having pretty good back issues training on the heavy rig without a suspension, and my chiropractor told me that if I kept training on that rig, I was going to put her kid through college! That is when I discovered the advantages of training the team with the ATV. With the ATV, I had much better control, and I could train a big team safely. A sixteen-dog team stretches over seventy feet long, which by comparison is about the same length as a tractor-trailer.

Mary Jo, Sarah, and I at a race in upstate New York

I was in heaven, running my dogs in the beautiful Pine Barrens on soft sand on a very comfortable ATV, with total control of the run and an unlimited number of miles and trails at my disposal. Well, that euphoria lasted about two weeks. One morning, as I was training a big string of dogs, I heard a siren. I looked behind me, and sure enough, there was a park ranger with lights flashing and sirens blaring, pulling me over. I stopped, and the ranger got out of his truck and walked up to me in amazement, taking in the sixteen-dog team barking and screaming to go (they really didn't care what he had to say). He told me that motorized ATVs were prohibited in the Pine Barrens. I told him I wasn't running the motor; the dogs were pulling it. I didn't even have the engine on because I didn't need it. He really didn't know what to say. As if on cue, my team said, *you guys can keep talking; we are going now*, and off they went! The team started dragging the ATV through the deep sand, and with the brakes firmly locked, rooster tails of sand were flying from each wheel. As I started to chase after them, I heard the ranger holler, "I will meet you back at your truck!"

I jumped on the ATV before they got too far from me, and then we continued our run, eventually making it back to the truck. While I was taking care of the dogs, the ranger pulled up and got out of his truck.

He shook his head and said, "That is the damnedest thing I have ever seen!" He had never seen a sled dog team before. He said although motorized ATVs *are* prohibited in the Pine Barrens, he admitted if we weren't running the engine, maybe he shouldn't consider it motorized. He explained the law was put in place because kids would race through the Pine Barrens on ATVs and crash, get seriously hurt, and then their parents would sue the state of New Jersey. Turned out I was lucky; this warden was the supervisor of that whole area, and he told me as long as I didn't run the motor, I could train on an ATV in the Pine Barrens. That was great news.

I trained in the Pine Barrens for the next twenty-five years. It is an amazing and beautiful place. I would occasionally see a hunter, but mostly, I was alone with my team and the abundant wildlife, especially deer. In my first few years, I never was able to train a team through those woods without seeing a half-dozen deer. I did have to be careful during the rutting season as the male deer occasionally got a little crazy (the rut is the deer breeding season, and a buck in rut can get aggressive). For a few years, I saw the same male deer with the biggest set of horns I have ever seen. I recognized him from one year to the next because his rack was very distinctive. I grew up in Ohio, so I have seen some big bucks, but this guy was the biggest one I have ever seen. In fact, I nicknamed him "The Hartford," after the insurance company's logo of a huge male elk. One day, he started getting way too close to my team during the rutting season. We were running through the Pine Barrens; The Hartford charged our team, and he ran alongside us for a bit before peeling off. A few days later, he ran right at us again but then stopped, his nostrils flaring and shaking his head. He charged us for a *third* time a couple of days later! He came from the side, heading towards our team like he was going to broadside us. He had his horns down and the tines heading straight for my leaders, but at the last minute, he lifted his head and leaped over the front four dogs in the team! It was startling for sure and pretty spectacular to consider after the fact. Some of the dogs practically laid down. I must admit, while it was happening, I was worried he was going to gore some of my dogs. I was glad for the timing: I was getting on a plane the next day and would be gone for a week for speaking engagements. This would give The Hartford time to settle down. I saw this big buck off and on for four years.

The wildlife that really got annoying during training sessions was the squirrels. It seemed like they wanted to play a continuous game of chicken, usually two of them at a time. They would literally run out of the woods in front of the team as we were approaching, look at us, and at the last second, jump up in the air and run back into the woods. More than once, our young leaders would follow them right into the woods, taking the whole team with them. It was great training for those young leaders. Once I got them trained to run uninterrupted past squirrels who seemingly looked like they were trying to commit suicide, they would run by anything. A few years ago, there was a commercial that depicted squirrel behavior exactly as what was happening to us. A car drove down the road, two squirrels would dart out in front of the car, the car slammed on its brakes, and tires squealed before the sounds of the car crashing into the woods. The camera would cut to the squirrels who were jumping up and down with excitement, high-fiving each other before they ran back into the woods. I really laughed the first time I saw it because of the memories of those squirrel encounters.

I noticed, over the years, the isolated Pine Barrens became a late-night party place for kids. While training, I would occasionally come by a pile of beer cans or bottles and a burned-out campfire. After training, I picked up any trash I could find and put it in a five-gallon pail in the back of my truck for recycling. I have always believed that when going into nature, you should try to leave it better than when you entered. One morning, I was on a training run as it was just getting light, and I could see a light up ahead of me on the edge of the woods. As I got closer, I could see an interior light shining from a car lying on its side on the edge of the woods. The driver obviously hadn't made the turn and rolled the vehicle. When we got near, I stopped the team, and I walked over to look into the car, expecting to see bodies. I was relieved to see the car was empty. A couple of days later, the car was gone, and as I was packing up my gear and the dogs, a ranger stopped by to tell me it was a stolen car that some kids had taken for a joy ride.

CHAPTER 16

◆

Driving to Alaska

After a few years of staying with friends for the winter in Alaska, we bought a ten-acre property from some good friends. The property had a mix of big pine and tall birch trees next to a slough that connected to the sled dog trail that wound for miles through pines, birches, and willows along the Tanana River. There was an old musher's cabin on the property, complete with a hole in the roof where a tree had fallen through, broken windows, and a foundation that had shifted so badly the door wouldn't open. A couple of red squirrels were living in it when we first arrived. It was a dry cabin, meaning there was no running water: there was an old outhouse next to it, which was also falling down.

Inside the cabin was a bed frame made from hand-hewn logs that, no doubt, were from the land on which the cabin was built. We bought the property for the location and access to the dog trails. The towering pines and birch trees promised we didn't have to worry about permafrost, a frozen layer on or under Earth's surface, often found in Arctic regions like Alaska, Greenland, Russia, and far northern portions of Eastern Europe. Trees don't grow well on permafrost, so if the trees in an area are very short or stunted, chances are there might be permafrost under the ground. Building on permafrost is

112

difficult because if the ground begins to thaw, it will resettle, and the foundation will begin to shift. This is certainly a big problem in parts of Alaska as the temperatures have begun to rise with climate change, and permafrost conditions are changing.

Our land was near Salcha, Alaska, in an area called "30 Mile." There are mileposts along most highways in Alaska, and the location of a property was often determined by the nearest highway milepost. So *30 Mile* was located thirty miles from Fairbanks. Located on the Old Valdez Trail, 30 Mile was established by dog mushers long ago when they couldn't even drive all the way into their cabins during summer. At the time, there was no bridge over the Piledriver Slough, and they would have to park on one side of the slough and use a boat to transfer goods, supplies, and dogs to their homes on the other side. Residents eventually set up a cable ferry, with a cable strung across the water from bank to bank and pulled by hand to move across the slough. The ferry held a metal cage large enough for a person or two and supplies to ferry across the slough. Once the slough froze over during the winter, residents could access their cabins by driving over the ice. In the early days, the area consisted of kennel after kennel of sled dogs, and at one time, there were more than six hundred dogs living in the area.

The Old Valdez Trail provided the first overland access to much of interior Alaska. Following a series of paths established by the indigenous people living there, it was built by the United States Army between 1898 and 1907 and upgraded to a wagon road in 1910 after the Fairbanks Gold Rush. It was gradually rerouted and became drivable by 1920. It was renamed Richardson Road and, eventually, Richardson Highway. Access to our cabin on the Old Valdez Trail is from the Richardson Highway, considered the oldest highway in Alaska. Part of our dog trail overlaps the original Old Valdez Trail, and I often thought, as I was cruising along with my dog team, how different life must have been in the late 1800s for people traveling virtually the same trail.

The drive to Alaska has changed a lot in my twenty trips up the Alaska highway, and by that, I mean the drive has *literally* changed.

Many of the tight switchbacks and curves have been straightened out as road improvements have been made. In fact, the drive has gotten more than a hundred miles shorter since the first time I drove the Alaska Highway. When I first did the drive back in the 1990s, there were still long sections of the highway that were gravel and not paved. In some ways, gravel was preferable because, in the winter, the snow would smooth out the roads, but some of the gravel would still make its way to the surface. With this gravel, you had good traction, and you could drive down the highway quickly. Once it became paved, the snow covering the road could often become slick and slow you down.

Alaska Highway, often snow-covered and slippery

My first drive up the highway was filled with trepidation and uncertainty. A 4,200-mile drive can be intimidating for sure. Add to the challenges of the long drive itself, being accompanied by twenty-five or so of your four-legged buddies who need to be let out of the truck for exercise, bathroom breaks, meals, and water about seven times per day. Also, this was before Garmin, GPS, and cell phones, so I had to be able to read road maps. Occasionally, I would find that my maps weren't always up to date. Reading a map is becoming a lost art with all the GPS systems available, but I have taught both my kids how to read maps (though I doubt either one carries a map in their car).

The trip to Alaska would take between seven and ten days, depending on the weather and whether or not I stopped to train dogs during the trip. One year, with weather delays and stopping to train, the trip lasted fourteen days. Most years, I left Pennsylvania in late November and returned in late March. One advantage of making these trips in the winter is that there is a lot less traffic. Many days, I might only see six other vehicles on the road all day. The downside of being on the road with so little traffic was if you broke down, you could freeze to death before help would arrive. During my early trips, it seemed somebody died every year somewhere on the Alaska Highway, either from a crash or exposure to the elements.

Road signs along the Alaska Highway that certainly get your attention

Another difficult part about driving the Alaska Highway in the winter was frost heaves, which can change from year to year. These are humps or depressions in the highway that are caused by permafrost melting or shifting. You can think of them as oversized speed bumps, and they can be scary as they can launch your truck into the air or break an axle if you're not prepared for them. Sometimes, you are traveling so fast that you don't see them until it is too late. I guess the condition of the Alaska Highway I was driving was still much better than the road the first mushers from the lower forty-eight faced.

Longtime champion sled dog racer Dr. Lombard and Ed Moody, who drove with him to Alaska in the late '50s, told me their road was so rough that they drove the highway with hard hats on because they were being bounced around so much.

It is a different story in the summer. Drives across the western portion of the Trans-Canada Highway onto the Alaska-Canada Highway is a steady stream of RVs. A lot of people call it the Alaska Highway, but it is more accurately called the Alaska-Canada Highway or the Alcan, as the locals refer to it. It starts in Canada at Dawson Creek, British Columbia, and runs 1,390 miles, ending in Delta Junction, Alaska. This is an absolutely beautiful portion of the drive I took so many times.

I don't remember all the details of the twenty drives I made to Alaska because, over time, they tend to blend in together. But I remember the first drive and how excited I was as I crossed into Alaska from Beaver Creek in the Yukon territory of Canada. Then, the realization hit me that I still had another three hundred miles left to get to Fairbanks. After being on the road for so many days, I was thrilled to finally be in Alaska—the mecca for sled dog sports. My dream had always been to race in Alaska, but I kept delaying it for one reason or another. One of my best friends, a champion dog musher from Alaska, finally said to me, "You know, if you wait until you think you have a good enough team to race here in Alaska, you will never come."

He was right. I was always making excuses. It had been a little intimidating to think about racing my team in Alaska against the best teams in the world while living about forty miles from Philadelphia. Sled dog racing in Alaska is like horse racing in Kentucky. It is the recognized state sport. My mind raced in a million different directions as I drove into Alaska for the first time. *Should I really be here? Is my dog team good enough to compete with the best in the world? How was my young family at home doing? I miss them so much!* Then, suddenly, *My gosh! Did I miss a turn?* I found myself driving on a narrow, twisty gravel road—I thought, *This can't be the famed Alaska highway!* Now, I had no idea what to do, and I did not have access to any rest areas, gas stations, or even road signs along the road. My only choice was to continue driving, hoping I would see a road sign that would help me figure out where I was. After what seemed like forever, I finally saw a car coming my way, and even better, it was an Alaskan State Trooper! I wasn't about to let him by, so I basically blocked the road. He stopped, rolled down his window, and gave me a quizzical look. I embarrassedly told him I must have made a wrong turn, and could he please direct me back to the Alaska Highway? He just started to laugh and said, "Well, young man, you are on it. Welcome to the Alaska Highway!" I was so relieved, and we both had a good chuckle.

I drove on until I found a place to pull off on the side of the road to let the dogs out. These were not the rest areas I was used to on Interstate 80 or the Ohio Turnpike. There were no buildings, no restrooms, or even signs—just a big, long parking area about twenty yards off the road. Some of the bigger stops might be about thirty yards wide and run close to one hundred yards long. These are called *roadside pullouts*—a place to park for road-weary drivers to pull off and get some rest. You could pull in on one end of the lot that paralleled the highway drive, park at any point, and then exit back onto the highway at the other end and be on your merry way. Occasionally, you would be traveling down the road and miss the first entrance into the pull-off (maybe the road was icy and you couldn't stop, or maybe it was on a curve and you didn't see it until too late), so you could turn into the second entrance, but when you did, now your vehicle was heading in the wrong direction when you left. Now, you have basically made a U-turn and are facing the opposite direction of traffic. If you pulled in to feed your dogs, let them out for some exercise, or even to take a nap, you could be in this pull-out for a while. So, when it is time to leave, you need to make sure you head down the road in the right direction. There are no signs like you'd see at a rest area in the lower forty-eight. As you pull out, there may be an arrow pointing one way for North and another pointing in the other direction for South. I got in the habit of turning my truck around right away if I had to enter at the wrong entrance to ensure I would always be heading in the right direction when I was finished.

I had a friend who learned this lesson the hard way. We were leap-frogging down the highway through the Yukon and into British Columbia. He had a handler with him to help with driving and caring for the dogs, and he didn't let his dogs out of the truck as often as I did. So, he would always get ahead of me. One day, I was letting the dogs out, and he flew by, going the wrong way! He saw me as he went by and realized that at the last pull-out, he had come out going the wrong direction because he knew I had been behind him. When he saw me, he realized he had gotten turned around on the Alaska Highway and lost about two hours of driving time.

The other thing to remember when driving the Alaska Highway in the winter is how many places close for the winter. There is not enough traffic to justify them staying open. Early on in my travels, many of these places were off the grid, so they depended on huge generators for electricity and heat. With high fuel costs, keeping a place operational in the winter becomes cost-prohibitive. As you are driving the highway in the winter, many of the gas stations, restaurants, and motels are buried in snow, and the driveway access is barricaded so you don't try to drive into them. These businesses make their money during the summer tourist season. Driving the road in the winter, the real problem becomes access to gas or diesel. In one section of the road, the distance between two open fuel stations was 250 miles. The other problem was that from year to year, you didn't know which fuel stations would be open. It got to the point that I thought about topping off my fuel tanks whenever I went by an open fuel center.

Meals were another concern. Many of these little villages or crossroads had one gas station, one restaurant, and a motel, and often were all in the same building. Early on, I learned that if you stopped for food at one of these one-horse locations, you should choose the daily special. The special would often be what the owner was feeding his family, and you would get generous, delicious portions. If you asked for something he had to take out of the freezer, it would be a longer wait and usually not that tasty.

The other thing you need to bring with you on this drive is your patience. I remember on one of my first trips I stopped for fuel, but when no one came out to my vehicle, I went into the building. A few people were sitting around the TV watching *Crocodile Dundee* on the VCR (that in itself should tell you how long ago this was!) A guy in coveralls looked up and said, "Can I help you?"

"Can I get some fuel?" I asked.

"Yep, I will be right with you," he said, then he went back to watching the movie for a few minutes until there was a slow part. Then he paused it, and he came out and pumped my fuel. It was not like I could go anywhere if I felt he took too long; the next fuel stop was more than a hundred miles down the road.

My first few trips were well before cell phones, and when you got onto the Alaska Highway, there really wasn't much for radio stations, so Sarah would make me CDs with my favorite music. She would act as a DJ between songs, which made portions of the trip very entertaining. When I got near some of the smaller villages, I would turn on my AM radio and hit search, and occasionally it would pick up a station. Often, I picked up nice Native music on these stations, but what was also entertaining to hear were the personal messages the radio DJ would read over the air for people living in the surrounding area without phone service. You would hear: "Jimmy Colbert, your mom wanted you to know your dad is in the hospital." Or something like, "Robert White, your sister had a baby boy. 8 lbs., 11 oz. Both are doing well." It was quite entertaining. Eventually, I started listening to books on tape while driving. I think I listened to every John Grisham book out there. Once they were widely available, cell phones made the trip much easier. Initially, I couldn't get cell service anywhere in Canada. Later, I was able to get service only around the bigger towns. On my last few trips, I had cell service the whole way.

I often get asked who drives with me to Alaska. Honestly, I didn't mind making the drive by myself. A 4,200-mile drive is a long time to be stuck in a vehicle with anyone. A few people have done the drive with me one way, and I think after they get out of the truck, they say that is enough; they are *one and done*. They can say they drove the Alaska Highway; they don't need to do it again on the way home.

Because my kids, Sarah and Alex, were in school, it was tough for them to do the drive with me. They would miss too much school, so instead, Mary Jo and the kids would fly up for a few weeks during the season. I would drive the dogs up, and then they would arrive. After the race season, they would fly home, and I would start the long drive back. I never worried about breaking down on the highway or driving through a bad storm when I was alone, but having my family with me in the truck made facing those same troubles a real concern.

We did have one memorable family drive to Alaska. On a typical drive to Alaska, I would get on the turnpike at Quakertown, PA, drive one hour north to Route 80, and head west through Chicago, up into Wisconsin, then through Minnesota and North Dakota, turn north into Canada onto the Trans-Canada Highway, to the Alaska Highway, and then to Salcha. Alex was about four years old at the time, and *Toy Story* was big then. Alex brought a Buzz Lightyear figure with him. He had no concept of how long the trip was going to be. Twenty minutes into the drive, he asked if we were almost there yet. I said no, not even close. After another twenty minutes, he asked again—same answer. After a half-hour, he asked *again*, and by now, I was getting a little annoyed with him. I sternly told him no, and I said, "Alex, I don't want you to ask me that again!"

A short while later, he says, "Dad."

"What, Alex?"

"Buzz has a question. He wants to know if we are almost there yet?" I almost came unglued. I looked at Mary Jo, and she was trying not to laugh, which didn't help! I think to myself, *Oh my, is this going to be a long, long trip!* Now, every time I think of that story, I can't help but laugh. We've shared this story countless times over the years at family gatherings, and it's become part of the family folklore.

We had to make special equipment adjustments to our trucks before driving to Alaska. One of the first was to ensure we chose an anti-freeze that would still work at temperatures as low as −65°F. I remember the first time I asked the dealer for this, they scoffed at it, saying that is not what the manufacturer recommends. I told them where I was going, and it was not a recommendation; it was a requirement. Of the trucks I owned over the years, I preferred diesel over gas because they got better mileage and had more power. Diesel trucks have (as standard features) engine block heaters with a cord to plug into an electric outlet to keep your engine warm overnight so it will start in the morning. When I purchased my last dog truck (a GMC), I asked the salesmen where the plug was for the block heater. He said this truck doesn't have one. I promised him it did. I finally convinced him to call the service manager, who came over and confirmed the truck did have one. The problem was we couldn't find it, and spent the next twenty minutes looking for it. The salesman had no idea these even existed, and no one had ever asked him about it. It may not be something many people in Southeastern Pennsylvania need to use. If you travel into northern climate areas like northern Minnesota, Canada, and Alaska, many parking lots, malls, or big box stores have electrical outlets at each parking spot. This allows you to plug in your car or truck when you are going to be in the store for a while.

On the front of the truck, we also mounted twin thousand-watt "moose lights" to light up the highway a long way ahead so you could see wildlife in enough time to safely stop. Wildlife on the road is one of your biggest concerns, especially at night. It is one thing to hit a squirrel or a rabbit; it is another thing to hit a 1,200-pound moose or a 1,500-pound bison. These lights are not something you would ever turn on in traffic as they would blind an oncoming driver. We also carried a spare fan belt and fuel filter as not every service station may have the one needed for your truck in stock, and replacement parts may take a week to get. In the truck, we carried a cold-weather sleeping bag, candles, plenty of water, and food, and on top of the truck, along with the sleds, we also packed a heavy-duty shovel.

In North America, the weather generally runs east to west. When you are heading from the East Coast, as I was while traveling to Alaska, if you hit a storm and keep going, you can drive through it. Of course, some storms are simply just not safe to drive through. One year, I got caught in a brutal storm just west of Edmonton, where I stayed in a hotel for three days, waiting for the weather to improve. With gale-force winds, cold temperatures, and heavy snow falling, it was simply not safe to be on the road. I was able to park the truck between the back of the hotel and a long trash dumpster to help cut the wind when caring for the dogs. The storm was blowing so hard that I couldn't feed the dogs outside of the truck, as the stainless-steel food bowls would blow away when I put them down on the ground. The dogs were plenty happy staying in the truck in their warm, comfortable straw beds, eating and sleeping while protected from the wind with heavy plastic louvers over the doors. Tragically, a husband and wife died during that storm just down the highway from where I had stopped to wait out the storm. In the prairies of Western Canada, a lot of the farms are well off the road, sometimes up to half a mile back. The driveways are very long, crossing open farm fields. Sadly, this couple, trying to make it home, got to their driveway, but it was all drifted in. So they left their car and attempted to walk to the house. The police are not sure if they got disoriented on the way, but their bodies were found when the storm calmed down about a hundred yards from the house. They both died of exposure.

Some of the worst storms I would encounter on the drive were the spring storms on my way back east from Alaska. One year after passing the Liard River Hot Springs in British Columbia, the snow started to pick up. The storm was getting worse, and it was getting late, so I thought it was maybe a good time to stop for the night. I was able to get a room at Muncho Lake. I woke up early the next morning to about seven inches of fresh snow on the ground but no plows on the road. I waited around until about 10:00 a.m. and decided I was heading out even though the road hadn't been touched by a plow or any other vehicle at that point. I reasoned that I had a big, heavy truck with all-wheel drive, so I wasn't worried. Frequently, in the Canadian Rockies, the snow might be heavy on one side of the mountain but be different when you cross over to the other side. That is exactly what happened this morning. I don't think I drove even ten miles down the other side of the mountain before there was almost no snow! I was excited that I could make up some time now.

A few miles later, a tractor-trailer was heading my way, and he was flying. As we head-on passed, one of his tires kicked up a stone that shattered my driver's side window. It sounded like a gunshot—boy, did I jump! The glass just fell on my lap and all over the floor, and of course, brought with it all the cold! I was able to find a place to pull off and started cleaning up the glass as best I could. I also removed the remaining shards of glass still attached to the window frame. Imagine driving your car in 10°F temperatures, at about sixty miles per hour, with your driver's side window wide open. I was freezing. I put on my insulated coveralls, my musher hat, and my mitts. I needed to find something to cover the window. Some of the pull-outs had trash dumpsters, so I stopped at each one to look in the dumpsters for something I could use. I never thought I would be a dumpster diver! Finally, I found a big piece of cardboard in one of them, and I used my knife to cut the shape I needed. I used duct tape, which I always carry, and taped up a cardboard window. It blocked the wind and some of the cold…but also eliminated my view, which is kind of nerve-wracking. I had 150 miles to go to get to Fort Nelson, where I hoped they would have a window, but when I got there, I was out of luck. I stayed with good friends, Terry and Debbie, that night, and they helped me redo my cardboard window by cutting a hole in the middle and taping in a clear plastic window so I could see a little bit out my side window. The closest replacement window I could find was in Fort St. John, another 250 miles down the road. I was able to get it replaced and stayed with other good friends, Ross and Tammy. In total, I had to drive about four hundred miles with no driver's side window.

The sled dog community is a tight group, and although during competitions, you are trying to win, everyone is pretty friendly and willing to help when they can. Early on in my travels to Alaska, before cell phones and the internet, traveling across Western Canada and through the Canadian Rockies, it was comforting to know I had great friends who would invite me into their house, make me feel at home, and allow me to get our dogs out for a run on their trails. Friends in Crooked Creek, Alberta, and in Fort St. John or Fort Nelson, BC, were very welcoming, and I will always remember their hospitality fondly.

For the most part, my twenty drives to Alaska were mostly free of truck mechanical problems. I only had two flat tires and a couple of clogged fuel filters, which were minor inconveniences, all things considered. I did have one issue and that was with a brand-new truck. When I left Pennsylvania, the odometer read 750 miles, and you can't get much newer than that. The trip was uneventful until eight days in. I was spending my last night in Canada, in Haines Junction, Yukon. I got up early the next morning and hit the road. I would be sleeping in my own bed at our cabin in Salcha, Alaska, that night. I only had about 470 miles to go—a relatively short day. By comparison, on a good day, I could drive more than 800 miles. The dogs would be happy to have the trip over and be out of the truck and stretching out in their heated log dog barn. I was excited, and no doubt the dogs could sense it as they seemed extra feisty that morning. We were about forty miles from the Alaskan border and the town of Beaver Creek, Yukon, when I pulled off to let the dogs run around and have a potty break. After all those years driving the highway, I learned the best places to stop and turn the dogs loose. It was cloudy and cold with a light snow falling. After a short break, I loaded everybody up and jumped into the truck to get back on the road. I started the truck, and as I hit the throttle to get back on the highway, there was a loud bang. The engine backfired, and it stalled. As I started it again, I got the following message on my dash: "Reduced Engine Power Warning." As I pulled out onto the highway, it didn't matter how hard I pressed the gas pedal; the truck would not go over twenty miles per hour. I worried it was a clogged fuel filter. I had one in the truck, but I remember a mechanic friend of mine who worked on these trucks warned me not to try and change it myself, as I had often done on my older trucks. He said I would really need a mechanic. I was hoping to find one in Beaver Creek.

03.25.2004

The majestic Canadian Rockies

It was a bit scary to go only twenty miles per hour down the highway as the big rigs were easily going three times faster. Would they see me in time to slow down? Even worse, we had to go through a hilly section with a lot of curves, and when we got to a hill, my speed slowed down to ten miles per hour. I was freaking out as I knew the tractor-trailers need a big head of steam to get up these hills, and they don't expect someone ahead of them to be going only ten miles per hour. I hoped that there wasn't any traffic coming up behind me. We finally made it to Beaver Creek around noon, and I found one mechanic open. I pulled up and walked in, but he didn't seem to be excited to see me. I told him I thought I needed a new fuel filter. He looked out at my truck and said he didn't have a fuel filter for that truck. When I told him I did, he said, "Well, I am going to lunch right now. Come back after 1:30, and I will look at it." Then, to make matters worse, a Royal Canadian Mounted Police (RCMP) officer walked in right then.

"Hi," the mechanic said.

"Hey Jim, I need to go to Whitehorse, and I need a new tire," the Mountie replied.

"No problem, I will do it right now," the mechanic responded. I realized then I was probably not going to get much help here. I went

125

out and sat in my truck, trying to decide what to do next. As I sat there, I thought, *Wait! I have OnStar; I can call them and see what they have to say.* Sure enough, they answered, called me by name, and said they were going to run a diagnostic on my truck. I am impressed! A few minutes later, the agent came back and told me what the problem was.

"Mr. Downey, your car should not be driven right now. We will send out a tow truck right away."

"Excuse me," I said, "do you know where I am located? The nearest dealer is three hundred miles from here, and they aren't even in the same country!" He was clueless. I thought, *Well, this won't work.* I said, "Thank you," and hung up. Then, I had another idea: I would use OnStar to call my dealer back in Souderton, Pennsylvania, and see if they had any suggestions. I got through to the service manager, and he said I could try one of two things: disconnect the battery or turn it off and on twelve times to reset the computer. I thought I would try turning it on and off first, as I was sitting in a warm truck. If that didn't work, I would get out in the cold and disconnect the battery. It worked, and I was happy to leave. I am sure the mechanic was happy to see me leave as well.

I made it all the way to Salcha under full power. I am not sure who was happier, me or the dogs! The next day, I called the dealership in Fairbanks and told him what happened. He said my truck would be fine and told me to bring it in next week. When I brought the truck in, he placed an eighteen-cent filter on a small vacuum tube by the engine. He said the manufacturer doesn't test their trucks in Alaska-type cold, and they deal with this a lot. My engine had sucked a tiny piece of ice into this vacuum tube which clogged it, and that caused the whole problem. He said their dealership installs them before any truck leaves the lot, but of course, that would not even be a consideration back in Pennsylvania. That problem has since been corrected by the manufacturer.

CHAPTER 17

Making a Home in Salcha

The original musher's cabin on the land we purchased in Salcha was uninhabitable, so we hired our good friend and neighbor, Eric, to build us a new cabin made from local spruce logs. The cabin was beautiful, including a circular log staircase leading upstairs to three small bedrooms. But it also had electricity and running water, something Mary Jo insisted on. Some women can be so demanding! The cabin had two large, triple-pane picture windows downstairs. One looked out over the dog yard and the dog barn. The other one looked out over the slough that ran alongside the cabin, about forty feet away, down an embankment.

Our warm, comfortable cabin in Salcha

Willows grew on either side of the slough all the way up to the cabin. We would occasionally watch moose feeding on the willows as we sipped our morning coffee. One day, we had a moose literally feeding on the willows just outside the window. Sarah and Alex were amazed watching her. I just couldn't get over how big she was. Of course, that was before the run-in I had with the moose.

Enjoying a meal of willows

Eric designed and built for us a heated dog barn on the banks of the slough, also made from spruce logs. We installed an air exchanger that was intended for fish rooms in northern climates. They are designed to remove humidity and stale air while conserving valuable heat, and this was certainly one of the best decisions we made in the design of the dog barn. This allowed the dogs to sleep in comfort in a warm building at night, whether it was 40°F above or 40°F below. The barn also protected them from the occasional moose that might wander through the dog yard or any wolf packs that might be in the area. One year, several pet dogs in our area were killed by a pack of wolves over the winter, but ours remained safe.

Our dog barn—a respite from the Alaskan cold and wildlife

A large fenced in area wrapped around three sides of the building. There was a divider down the middle to create two big exercise areas. There was a big gate that you could leave open, so the dogs had the run of both sides. We had a door on each side of the dog barn, so when that gate was closed, you could let some dogs out one door into one area and then let some dogs out the other door into a separate area. Often, we would let males out on one side and females out on the other. The dog barn also had two rooms; one side had the heater, where we could dry equipment or wax sleds, and the other side held the dogs. Each dog had an individual kennel with plenty of room to stretch out and relax. Someone once asked how we kept weight on our dogs when the temperature was as low as −50°F. The truth is we were actually concerned about them *gaining* weight at those temperatures. When it is that cold, they stay in the barn and stay warm. I let them out for bathroom breaks throughout the day, but they run out, do their business, and run back into the barn.

Alex lets the dogs out at night; they are always happy to see him!

I typically did not train when it was any colder than −20°F. Occasionally we would have week long streches where the weather was predicted to drop to at least −40° at night. If it warmed up to −20°F during the day I would train a team. I would hook a small team, say a six-dog team, and take them only on a six-mile run. To minimize the time they would be out in the cold, I would get the sled and the lines all laid out ahead of time. I would let the six dogs I was going to train outside for a quick bathroom break before we trained. When they returned to the barn, I would put ointment on every paw so they wouldn't build up with ice and get fissures. I would put their harnesses on and then a Lycra running suit. A couple of dogs had short hair on their ears, and I was worried about frostbite, so they also got a Snood, which is like a neck warmer that comes up over their ears to protect them. I then let them out the main door, and they would run to the sled. I hooked them up, and we took off. About eighteen minutes later, we would be back at the barn. I turned them loose, and they ran back into the barn. Inside, I took off their running gear, gave them some water and treats, and then moved on to the next six dogs. I repeated this routine three or four times some days. Afterward, I was exhausted, and not to mention a little chilled. While the dogs were only out in the cold and on the trail for eighteen minutes, I was out in the cold for hours.

In addition to the new cabin, we also had the original musher's cabin on the property rebuilt as the logs were still in good shape. With a new roof, new windows, and a new floor, it made for a great guest cabin. It contained an old table I used while I worked on Annamaet formulas there in the woods. In fact, Annamaet Salcha, Aqualuk, and Manitok were originally formulated in that cabin.

The original mushers' cabin, post-renovation

We had friends stay in it for a while every season. During some of those years, our good friend Ralph came up from Virginia and spent time there to help us with the dogs. Many of our Alaskan friends were more than captivated by his southern accent. I still chuckle, thinking about a great meal we had at a neighbor's home. After dinner, Ralph thanked her, saying, "Well, that meal was finer than frog's hair!"—not a comment you'd typically hear in Alaska. The guest cabin was still a dry cabin, so it had no running water and no bathroom. While we rebuilt the cabin, the existing outhouse was beyond repair. So, the nearest bathroom was in our cabin, over one hundred yards away— not nearly as convenient as the willows surrounding the guest cabin. One cold night, Ralph said he went out to the edge of the porch to relieve himself. When he looked up, he was face-to-face with a moose eating willows. Ralph said he jumped and ran back into the cabin, almost peeing on himself as he did. He said from that night on, he always turned on the yard lights when he went out after dark. I still laugh just thinking about it.

Spending winters in that log cabin was truly magical. We all have fond memories of our time in Alaska at the cabin. When Alex was only about six years old, we spent the day racing at an Alaska Dog Mushers Association (ADMA) preliminary race in Fairbanks. Alex was running around outside with his friends all day in the cold. When we got home, we took care of the dogs first. Alex was no doubt very tired but still wanted to stay outside and play down on the slough. Suddenly, Mary Jo hollered for me from the kitchen to go check on Alex as he was lying motionless on the ice. I threw my boots on and ran out there, only to realize he had gotten so tired he had fallen asleep right on the snow-covered ice. We still chuckle about it.

One day, I was training three eight-dog teams, which meant I would be out there for a while. It was early in the year, so we didn't have much daylight. I waited for the temperatures to warm up, which meant I started later in the day, and while I was out with the last team, it started to get dark. I could still see where we were going as we came home, turned onto the slough, and headed back towards the dog barn. We came by the cabin, and the lights of the cabin shining through that big window produced such a beautiful glow down towards the slough that it really warmed my heart. I will forever remember that moment. Recently, I found a painting of a similar scene of a dog team heading up a river toward the glow of a log cabin. That painting now hangs in my office.

-50 is serious cold!

I have another vivid memory of the cabin from one early morning when a serious ice fog meant we wouldn't be training. I was out in the dog barn working on a sled when I glanced out the window and saw a moose meandering up from the slough towards a training sled aimed at the dog barn. It had been left behind after a training run the day before. The moose seemed to be intrigued with the sled; she made her way right up to it and even sniffed it. She stood there with her front hooves next to my runners. From where I was standing, it looked like she was standing on the runners, just like I do. She lifted her massive head and looked left and then to the right—it was so impressive! Unfortunately, my phone was in the cabin on the charger.

But I have that portrait permanently etched in my mind. It was made even more dramatic by her being draped in ice fog—it really made her look a little spooky.

We had twenty amazing winters living in Alaska with our dogs. Our life in Alaska wasn't always about racing; we also made some lifelong friends and cherish the time we had together. Our friends used to needle us that we had it backward: they said we spend our summers in the heat and humidity of the East Coast and our winters in the Arctic. They said it would be a lot better to spend our summers in Alaska and our winters on the mild East Coast. I wanted to say that we get some nasty winters on the East Coast, but I'm sure I would get laughed at saying that to someone who, after a week at −40°F, was looking forward to a sunny day with temperatures warming up to −30°F, and that is air temperature, not wind chill. Summers in Alaska are spectacular for sure, especially if you like constant daylight. In fact, every year, they play the Midnight Sun Baseball Game in Fairbanks on June 21, the summer solstice. The festivities start at 10:00 p.m. with no artificial lights. They tell you to bring your sunglasses and grab a seat. Just before midnight, they take a break, and instead of singing "Taking Me Out to the Ballgame," they sing "Alaska's Flag" song. Alumni of the game include Major League Baseball royalty such as Tom Seaver, Dave Winfield, Terry Francona, Harold Reynolds, and Jason Giambi.

One year, we were invited to the outdoor wedding of our good friends Dan and Debbie, who lived just up the road. The wedding was in March in Salcha. The location was about six miles along the Tanana River near an old trapper's trail that has become part of our dog mushing trails. In mid-March, the average temperature is a low of −1°F, and the high is a balmy 24°F. The average snow depth at this time of year is fifteen inches. The only way to get to the wedding was by snowmobile or dog team. Because our dogs were crazy racing dogs, we figured they wouldn't sit quietly during the ceremony. We were sure they would be barking and carrying on. We decided to go in by snowmobile using our old Skidoo Tundra. The Tundra was a trusted and very light-work snowmobile favored by trappers throughout

Alaska and Canada. Its engine was simple to work on and light enough to move around if you got stuck in the snow. Ours was a 1985 model with no reverse, but it started great almost every time.

At the time, Alex was seven, and Sarah was fourteen years old. Mary Jo sat behind me on the snow machine, and we had a tow rope that pulled a junior dog sled that Alex rode on, and then the rope continued to an adult dog sled that Sarah rode. On the way to the wedding, we took our time and stopped and looked at wolf tracks, then we stopped and looked at moose tracks, and we even stopped at one point at a curve in the river with rapids that had open water to see if there was any grayling—a popular sport fish that often could be found in the interior Alaskan rivers.

The wedding was special. It was outside in a beautiful forest of tall pines along the river. The river had some open rapids at the site, so the wonderful sound of running water provided a backdrop during the event. They had a bonfire for heat and lawn chairs set up with caribou hides covering them for warmth.

The bride arrived by dog team from one direction in a wedding gown and mukluks; the groom arrived by dog team from the other direction wearing insulated Carhartt coveralls, typical clothing for the interior of Alaska. The wedding was a beautiful event! Unfortunately, Mary Jo was not feeling well and had a fever, so as soon as the ceremony was over, we had to leave. We got back on the snow machine, the kids got back on their sleds, and we started heading home. Because Mary Jo was sitting behind me, her job was to keep an eye on the kids as we were towing them back. Off we went for the slow ride back home. I couldn't go very fast as we were pulling the kids on dog sleds. I noticed after a while that Mary Jo's head was resting on my shoulder. A while later, I glanced over my shoulder to see how the kids were doing. *Oh my God! No kids! Just two empty sleds! What could have happened to them*, I wondered, *Did they fall into the river? Did a moose charge them? Could it have been the wolf whose tracks we were looking at on the way in?* I was in a panic. I slammed the snowmobile to a stop, which woke Mary Jo up, and she screamed, "Where are the kids!" I hollered back, "I don't know, you were supposed to be watching them!"

Because it was a narrow, old trappers' trail, I didn't take time to turn the snow machine around; I just started running down the trail looking for them. I thought they must be just around the bend! I ran the first straightaway around that curve: no kids! I ran the second straightaway around the bend: no kids! By now, I was really scared. Finally, I ran the third straightaway, and around that curve, I saw at the far end of the straightaway (about one hundred yards away) our daughter Sarah, standing in the deep snow off the side of the trail holding Alex, just as others were passing from the wedding! Someone asked, "Where are your Mom and Dad?" Sarah replied, "I don't know, they just went that way," pointing down the trail.

What a relief they were found, but how did it happen, and was anyone hurt? It turned out that Alex, being a typical seven-year-old, was playing around on his sled, sliding back and forth. He caught a rut in the trail, which flipped him in the air, and he fell off his sled. Sarah, who was behind him on her sled, got pulled over his legs: even today, when they are both adults, Alex still likes to say she did it on purpose! When it happened, they both started screaming, but I could not hear them because of the noise of the snowmobile. Mary Jo was out of it, so she didn't see or hear anything. Alex was being left behind, lying in the snow as we continued down the trail. Sarah decided she couldn't leave her little brother out there alone and jumped off her sled to stay with him, figuring that at some point, we would notice they were missing.

After we were reunited with the kids and everything was okay, then the humor of the situation took hold.

"Dad, what took you so long to come back for us?" Sarah asked.

"Well, sweetie," I said, "I had to convince Mommy we should come back for you!" That night at the wedding reception, word sure got around about our little *faux pas*. Boy, did they give us a hard time! I kept hearing, "Honey, I lost the kids!"

CHAPTER 18

Racing in Alaska

The races I entered most frequently were sprint races up to sixteen-mile heats. Most races were two or three-day events. Calling a sixteen-mile run a sprint may sound a bit odd to someone not familiar with the sport, but there are even thirty-mile races that are considered sprints. I would usually race in the eight- or ten-dog class, which is the maximum number of dogs in the team. I also raced in the "unlimited" or "open class," as it is often called, meaning you can run as many dogs as you choose to put in your team. In those races, I would typically run fourteen or sixteen dogs. Sixteen miles was my self-imposed limit, as I always felt any dog we had could be conditioned and trained train to run sixteen miles comfortably. Beyond that distance, I felt the physical limitations of some dogs might prevent them from running further without having trouble. Our dogs were like family members. Some of our dogs simply couldn't race longer distances, and they would have to be replaced—something that our family simply wasn't willing to do. So we never competed in the two biggest sprint races in Alaska: The Open North American Championship in Fairbanks, which has two 20-mile heats and one 30-mile heat; or the Anchorage Fur Rendezvous' which has three 25-mile heats. I was ridiculed by some for not competing in these longer distances, but that is their issue, not mine. I was comfortable with my decision and wasn't going to be pressured. Besides, success in racing has never been that important to me. I just really loved spending time with our dogs and allowing them to enjoy what they do. People have no idea how much these dogs love being sled dogs.

As a result of my training in the sciences, I have been keeping journals since I was in college. In writing this book, I went back and read all of them, which really brought back memories, some good and some not so good. However, I was able to establish that I had owned sled dogs for thirty-eight years and was on the back of a dog team more than six thousand times while covering over forty-two thousand miles, which is almost twice the circumference of our planet! I have friends who certainly have done more than I have. Considering that we live near Philadelphia, where the average temperature in mid-October is 65°F, I don't think that's too bad. I have competed in sled dog races in sixteen American states and six Canadian provinces. I was also fortunate enough to be invited to be the first United States musher to compete in a sled dog race in Argentina. That was an amazing trip, boarding a plane in New York City on a hot (summer) August day and arriving on a snowy August (winter) day in Ushuaia, Argentina, at the southern tip of South America.

A big key to our ability to get a dog team ready to race in Alaska while living outside of Philadelphia was the use of a modified horse walker. We would train our dogs on the wheel for up to three hours a day. This slow, moderate conditioning was key for us establishing a competitive dog team. You can help your dog's ability to work for longer periods in the heat by moderate continuous training like this. Many people want to go out and train fast with each run, but I have always believed a dog team only has so many fast runs in them during the season. If you use them up in training, the ability won't be there on race day.

We built the surface up around the wheel with rubber mulch like they use in playgrounds. It really made for soft, safe footing for the dogs. I was surprised by how much the dogs loved it—every dog we had loved the wheel. Other people who tried using a wheel had dogs that simply hated it, but that was never the case for us. One day, Mary Jo and I came home from the office and couldn't believe what we saw. Spirit, a retired dog who was fourteen years old at the time, was loose, and she was just trotting around the wheel all by herself—without a care in the world. All we could do was laugh. We have recently repurposed the wheel, and now we hang swings from it in the summer, and it has become a great merry-go-round for our grandsons. In the winter, they use it with sleds or snowboards if we have any snow.

The year Mary Jo ran in the Women's Fur Rendezvous, I raced in a few open races in Anchorage, Willow, and Montana Creek near Talkeetna, better known as the jumping-off point for climbers hoping to summit Denali, North America's tallest peak. In Anchorage, I raced in the Orville Lake Classic, which had a big, competitive field. I was in the rookie draw at the back of the pack, and I raced sixteen dogs, with Taiga and Ten in lead. Taiga was Ten's sister, about the same size and all black. She could be a little sensitive, and honestly, I don't think she would have been a good leader for many people, but we had a connection, and she trusted me. It had started to snow heavily as the first team left the chute.

By the time I took off, there was more than five inches of fresh snow on the trail, and I could hardly see my leaders. But I quickly noticed that Jodi, my superstar point dog, had left the chute tangled, with her line wrapped around her back leg. I certainly couldn't let her run like that for the next twelve miles, but it was going to be hard to stop and hook down an excited race team just after starting, especially in all that fresh snow. I had no choice. If I kept going, Jodi was really going to get hurt. I stood on the brake with both feet and when I finally got them to stop, I slammed a snow hook into the fresh snow on each side of the sled. I jumped on each one, trying to push it down into the hard-packed base under all the new snow. They held as I was able to run up alongside the team and untangle Jodi, but then the hooks popped, and the team took off as I was trying to get back to the sled. The snow hooks were each shooting up rooster tails about four feet in the air as they dragged along, trying to hold the team, but there was too much loose snow on top.

I dove into the team and grabbed the center gang line that ran from the leaders to the sled. Somehow, it formed a half hitch around my wrist, and I was being dragged down the trail on my back. I didn't have to worry about losing the team anymore, as there was a knot around my wrist, and I couldn't have let go if I'd wanted to. This was spooking the dogs a bit as I was flopping around in the middle of the team, and they had to avoid stepping on me as we went down the trail. This was progressing into a dangerous situation. The pain in my wrist was unbelievable, but at least I was still with the team. I knew that in about another mile and a half, we would be coming to a tunnel that ran under a busy road, and there would be trail help there who would assist me. (In Anchorage, as the city grew in population and traffic, they started putting tunnels under road crossings so everyone using recreational trails would not have to cross the roads; they would just go under them.) Dragging alongside my team, I didn't realize that the snow was finally slowing down. We soon came into an area that had heavy tree cover, which meant less snow was hitting the ground in the first place, so there was not as much loose snow on top of the packed trail. Suddenly, the hooks caught, and the team slammed to a stop! The half hitch got ripped off my wrist, which I thought for sure broke it. My glove flew off to the side, and I got up and ran back to the sled. Now, the snow hooks were really deep, and I had a hard time getting them out of the hardpack. This all happened in the first mile—we still had eleven to go! I grabbed my glove as we went by, and the dogs ran great the rest of the way; no more drama! On Sunday, I only took fourteen dogs with me, and we had a nice, clean run. The dogs cut more than three minutes off our time. No doubt, most of that time difference on day one was the dogs having to drag my fat butt down the trail on my back.

I have been fortunate enough to compete in sled dog races for twenty years in Alaska against the finest dog teams on earth. It is, by far, the best competition in the world. I have won a few of the top races there and lost many, many more, but I will always remember my first race in Alaska. It was in the small Athabascan village of Tanacross, with a population of under 150 people. It is located just off the Alaska Highway, about ten miles west of Tok. The race began at noon on a Saturday, and I had a hard time sleeping that Friday night. I got to the race site Saturday morning, and as I started getting all my gear set up, I looked around and began getting more nervous. *Should I even be here? Have I trained the dogs enough?* I couldn't help but notice all the big-time dog mushers who were there to race as well—guys I have read about but never met. It felt like playing in a golf tournament and realizing I was going up against Tiger Woods and Scottie Scheffler.

Finally, it was race time. This waiting around was nerve-wracking. I just wanted to get out on the trail with my dogs, and I would be fine. I had my race bib on, my sled all set up, my lines laid out, and the dogs were ready, harnessed, and raring to go. As I was about to start hooking up my first dog, this big guy came over, looked down at me, and asked, "So, who are you?"

"Rob Downey," I replied.

"Where are you from?" he asked.

"Pennsylvania."

"So what are you doing here?" he asked.

"Well, hopefully, I am going to race."

He looked me right in the eye and said, "This is my race; you'd better be good!"

I couldn't believe it. I drove over four thousand miles to listen to some trash talk! I think my team and I surprised a few people because I finished in the top five on the first day. On Sunday, as I was getting ready to hook up my team, the guy who had given me a hard time the day before came over and offered to help me get my team into the chute. I couldn't help but think that was his way of saying, *Welcome to Alaska, young man from Pennsylvania! I guess I misjudged you!*

They call the North American Championship the "Granddaddy of them all." The race has been around since 1946, though sled dog racing in Fairbanks has been a tradition since 1927. The North American Championship has evolved over the years and now includes two separate races: The Open North American Championships and the Limited North American Championships. The only difference is whether there is a limit to the size of your dog team. The Limited has classes for eight-, six-, and four-dog teams and now even includes two-dog skijoring. My focus was always on the eight-dog class. This race is also three days, with heats that used to be twelve miles on each of the first two days and fourteen miles on the third. (They have since cut it to 10.5 miles on the first two days and twelve miles on the third day.)

My goal was to win the eight-dog Limited North American Championship. Not an easy task! One challenge for me is that everyone competes equally in sled dog sports, regardless of gender, size, or weight, and in the eight-dog class, you are limited to eight dogs. I am six feet tall and weigh just north of two hundred pounds. I often compete with other drivers who may be five feet, four inches tall and may weigh only one hundred twenty pounds soaking wet. This puts me at a definite disadvantage, so I tended to include bigger dogs in my team to help compensate for my size.

I had a lot to learn about racing in the Limited North American Championship (LNAC). The trail was usually pristine, very well groomed, and very fast. I found that my training in the soft sand in the New Jersey Pine Barrens really muscled up my dogs and made them tough. When I got to Alaska, we needed at least two weeks of training to stretch out their muscles so they could run fast. It was a learning curve. Over the years, I worked my way up from the back of the pack at the LNAC to the middle of the pack to the top three in the last few years of my racing career. I was not quite able to pull off the win—close but no cigar!

The year I got stomped by the moose could have been our year. I was undefeated in the preliminary race season, and everything looked like it was our time. Then I got stomped by the moose, and my season was over. The recovery was long and arduous. I had two surgeries on my elbow and wasn't allowed to leave Alaska for six weeks. When we finally headed down the highway, I was allowed to drive, but I couldn't handle the dogs: doctors' orders. Mary Jo had to let them (all twenty-five of them) in and out of the truck seven times a day. It didn't help that I followed her around, offering suggestions on how to do it better—or at least, how to do it my way! She would just suggest I stay in the truck and get some needed rest. We look back on it now and laugh at how difficult that trip turned out to be. I don't do well with downtime. Mary Jo was more than qualified to handle the dogs; just because she didn't do things my way didn't mean it was the wrong way! I can be too much a creature of habit.

I had a lot of time to ponder my future on that drive home. One thing I knew was that I would be back next year racing dogs in Alaska as I had for the last fourteen years. Many people thought I would stop, but they don't know me: I am usually not smart enough to quit. Besides, I knew this was the best dog team we ever had, and they deserved another shot at the Limited

North American Championship.

*Mary Jo, Alex, and Mic on the drive home, as they
had to care for the dogs the whole trip*

The next season, which was 2005, I was healed except for the bolt and wire in my elbow (still in there today) and headed back to Alaska. Everyone asked me what I would do the next time I saw a moose. I told everyone I wasn't worried, but to be honest, I was not sure how I would react. Even today, I can remember the particular, musty smell of that moose, a smell that I think will always be with me. I also learned that our run-in with the moose had a big effect on one of our dogs as well. You may remember that the day I got stomped by the moose started off very cold—it was −35°F when I got up that morning, and I don't train dogs at those temperatures. However, because it was going to remain that cold for a while, I decided to run the young dogs, who had been off for a couple of days. By 1:00 p.m., it had warmed up to a balmy −20°F. I decided to train a team of young dogs and headed out on the trail. I had an older veteran dog, Satin, in lead. A little grey dog, she had been an amazing lead dog for us for many years. But at this point, she was happily running with our yearlings as she was bossy, and I think she enjoyed pushing them around. Next to Satin in lead was Mac, a big black and white male who was colored like a Holstein cow. He was only a yearling, but I really thought he was going to be our next great leader. After the moose incident, he had no interest in running in front of the team. He would do it, but you could tell he didn't like it. You could put him in the team anywhere but in lead, and he was as excited to run as ever. Put him in lead, though, and he would literally start shaking. Once I realized this, we made the easy decision never to put him in lead again. I was really surprised by his reaction as I have always thought that dogs live in the moment.

Throughout the season, training was going very well; the dogs were all happy and healthy, and the team was really looking good. I did not see any moose out on our runs, which was unusual. I usually saw them off in a meadow as we went by, feeding on the tall grass that came up through the snow or on the willows that lined the trail. But this time, I trained for several weeks and never saw a single moose! It was starting to get into my head! *Where were they?* Finally, one chilly morning on a training run, I was out on the trail even farther than when I got stomped, and it was like déjà vu all over again! I turned off the main trail, and as I began rounding a turn, there was a big cow moose on one side of the trail, and on the other side was her calf! We were heading right in between them!

Do you know how I reacted? I slammed on the brakes and screamed like a baby, "AAAAAGGHH!"

Well, luckily, it was last year's calf, and Mom wasn't as protective as she would have been for a newborn, so she ran off. I was able to slam on the brakes and stop the team, and the yearling calf crossed in front of us, chasing after Mom! I laughed all the way back to the cabin, thinking, *Yeah, you are a real tough guy!*

It was a good race season for us. The team was still getting better, in large part because they were a little young. This was the season they came into their own. I won the two Challenge Series races I entered but still only finished third in the Limited North American Championships.

The next year, 2006/2007 was a great season for us. We competed in a few races in the lower forty-eight and headed to Alaska at the end of January, feeling pretty good about our team. Our leaders, a pair of brothers named Vinnie and Veto, were nicknamed "the South Philly Boys," a combination of our living near Philadelphia and the popularity of "The Sopranos" (the TV series about a New Jersey-based mob boss). We'd had some amazing individual lead dogs over the years, dogs like Salt, Jessie, Ten, and Bow, but Vinnie and Veto were the best pair of leaders we ever had. I say pair because neither was individually the finest of lead dogs, but together, they were the best for sure. I could drive Vinnie like a car: tell him to turn right, and he would turn right. If the trail was better on the left side, I could ask him to move to the left, and he would. Veto, on the other hand, had little interest in listening to commands. Wherever Vinnie wanted to go, Veto was good with that. Veto's strength was in his drive: he wanted to go at full speed all the time. It was all or nothing with him. That wasn't always a good thing if the trail was tough or if it was a warm day. I really had to work at holding him back, or he would run the rest of the team into the ground. Veto was built like a canine athlete should be—well-balanced, light on his feet, poetry in motion. He set an amazing pace, and it was easy for him to run that fast. Vinnie, on the other hand, was big and blocky, with a square head and big feet! He would pound down the trail. You could not run anybody with either of them as they both had attitude and intimidated every dog you tried to run next to them—except each other.

Vinnie and Veto, the South Philly Boys
Photo credit: Dave Partee

Standing in the chute, they would go crazy with excitement—chewing, barking, and snapping at each other. It never escalated to a serious dog fight. They seemed to know how far they could push each other—something I guess that is typical of any set of brothers. Running in lead is a lot of pressure, so most mushers will train with their race leaders back in the team occasionally to take the pressure off. Vinnie and Veto would not tolerate running back in the team. I think they felt it was beneath them, often intimidating the dog I was trying to run lead. They ran lead every day they trained or raced. I always said when it was time for them to retire, they would have to retire together, and that was what we did.

ADMA ten-dog Gold Run Championships
Photo credit: Dave Partee

That season, we ended up winning the International Sled Dog Racing Association Gold Medal in both the eight-dog and ten-dog classes. This is an overall world ranking for the season. The highlight of the year was winning the Alaska Dog Mushers Association Black Gold Championship Race in Fairbanks. We also had another third-place finish in the Limited North American Championship as well as the Tok Race of Champions.

A warm fall on the East Coast forced me to leave for Alaska at the beginning of December 2007 to get ready for the race season of 2008. Mary Jo and the kids planned to fly up for the holidays. We always enjoyed Christmas in Alaska as those were special times. For one thing, we were pretty much guaranteed a white Christmas, and that was always appreciated. One new tradition for us was the frequent fireworks displays we saw on New Year's Eve. Alaskans couldn't enjoy them on the Fourth of July as it never got dark enough to see them. So, the big fireworks displays were saved for New Year's Eve.

Pretty much a guaranteed white Christmas every year in Salcha, AK

I changed my training philosophy a bit for this season. I now had a veteran team, and I didn't think they needed to have as many longer runs on them. I wanted them to go into the racing season fresh. They got added rest when the temperature hit –45°F for a week early in February and stayed close to that for six days. We don't train in those temperatures!

By the time March rolled around, those –45°F temperatures were a distant memory. Mary Jo had flown up to help us at the Limited, and having her there was so important as we are a good team, and a team always functions better when it is complete. It had become warm, and the conditions were tough. I thought this was a real advantage for us. As I mentioned, I tended to select bigger, stronger dogs, and thanks to training and living in Pennsylvania, warm weather didn't bother them. They thrived in it. My team was made up of eight male dogs with an average weight of sixty-two pounds each. We probably weren't the fastest team in the race, but I think we were the toughest. Day one of the Limited North American hit 48°F, which is very warm for interior Alaska. It is better suited for a team coming from the

Mid-Atlantic area on the East Coast. My plan that day was to hold the team back and not let Veto run them into the ground or take too much out of them in these warm temperatures. I knew any team that went too hard on day one would pay for it on days two and three. We were in second place after day one. *Did I hold them back too much?* I wondered.

Day two was cooler but still in the high 30's. A couple of teams wore out after running in close to 50°F on day one. Our team just seemed to get stronger and we moved into first place. By day three, our team was just rolling around the trail. I could tell by the way they were running no one was going to catch us! One of the things that I always found amazing in my sled dog career is that when your team was moving at maximum efficiency, none of the lines were tight. All the lines are loose, like no dog is pulling, but you are just flying down the trail, dogs as happy as can be! I was able to just enjoy the ride, and I felt these dogs knew they were winning as well. They just cruised up that last hill back to the finish line.

Our winning team in the Limited North American,
led by Vito and Vinnie, the South Philly boys
Photo credit: Dave Partee

I had a hard time stopping them when I got back to the truck. They were still barking, ready to go; they wanted more! I had to fight back the emotions; this was the goal I had worked hard to accomplish for so many years. My family made a lot of sacrifices to get us here. And finally, I was going to win the Limited North American Championships. The mushing community is a tight group: while out on the trail, you are trying to win, but after the race, you are all still friends. A bottle of Champagne was put on the hood of my truck by friends; we popped it and celebrated! There were many toasts. I can't tell you how relieved I was to finally reach my goal, and I was so thankful I had Mary Jo there to celebrate with me.

Because sled dog racing is the recognized state sport in Alaska, the top sports stars are dog mushers. It gets plenty of coverage in the press. The next day, I opened the *Fairbanks News Miner, and the sports headline read,* "Downey Finally Wins North American." Ouch!

CHAPTER 19

◆

Racing with the Whole Family

We are often asked how we got the kids out of school for so long. Our lifestyle wouldn't have worked without the flexibility of the small parochial school they attended—St. Agnes in Sellersville, Pennsylvania. Sarah and Alex had amazing teachers there who thought it would be a great learning experience for them. Their teachers also thought it would be great to connect their school to the school in Salcha they'd be attending. Of course, our kids had to keep their grades up, or they wouldn't be able to go to Alaska. They took schoolwork with them while also attending Salcha Elementary. It was small enough (about sixty children) that it housed two grades per classroom. Once they hit junior high, they would go to school at the Eielson Air Force Base just southeast of Moose Creek, Alaska, about twenty-six miles from Fairbanks. At Salcha Elementary, they went out for recess every day unless there was a moose in the schoolyard or it got colder than −20°F.

Every Tuesday at Salcha Elementary, from January to March, the students had the opportunity to get involved with the Salcha Ski Club's youth cross-country ski program, where they maintain fifteen kilometers of trails. The ski club even provided skis, poles, and ski boots. Alex really wanted to do it, so he signed up. He had never been on skis before, and it showed. It was like the tortoise and the hare; he was so slow, and the other kids would just fly by him. But everyone was great about it, encouraging him, helping him up when he fell—which was often! If you know Alex, you know how hardheaded he is (Mary Jo prefers "determined"). He didn't quit; he just kept getting better. Every few weeks, they would have a race, and although for the first couple of races, he was finishing way behind his cohort, by the end of the year, he was bringing home medals.

When the kids attended Eielson AFB for Junior High, they got to select one elective class between Wilderness Survival, Art and Music, Tech and Computer, Home Economics, or Physical Education. They obviously both chose Wilderness Survival, a course not offered back in Pennsylvania. Sarah learned how to start a fire using only sticks in the snow. I was pretty impressed when she did it at our cabin. Alex learned how to make a figure-four deadfall trap out of wood that his teacher told them "could snap the neck of a moose." He built one at the cabin and did a really good job with it. Thankfully, no animals were hurt during this homework project!

Jeff Studdard Race Ground, Fairbanks, Alaska

Both Sarah and Alex grew up with dogs, so it came as no surprise when they both expressed interest in racing with them. Sarah competed in her first sled dog race as a two-year-old running a friend's

Jack Russel terrier in a kid-and-mutt race in Saranac Lake, New York. When she got a little older, about eight years old, she was excited to race in Alaska. On day one of this three-day championship race, she was nervous, but probably not as much as her mom and dad.

We were at the Jeff Studdert Racegrounds in Fairbanks, home of the Alaska Dog Mushers Association. The ADMA was started in 1948 to promote dog mushing, dog racing, the humane treatment of dogs, and especially, the North American Championships. They have been hosting club events ever since. Sarah was competing in the Junior North American Championships. We were confident in the two dogs she was running, both older dogs who may have been past their prime but still loved to race and had been around these trails dozens of times. Sarah was basically raised with these dogs, and she knew and trusted them completely. In fact, the one challenge we foresaw was that the trail was only a mile long, which, to these dogs, would be like a warm-up! They really liked running farther. Eight to twelve miles was more in their sweet spot. We were glad a race official would be at the turnaround to make sure Sarah was heading back to the clubhouse, just in case they got carried away.

Before the two-dog class started, it was reported that a moose was out on the trail down in the birch trees, feeding off the willows near the trail. This was a concern not only for parents but also race officials. Quickly, the race marshal set off on a snowmobile down the trail with a high-powered rifle slung over his shoulder to make sure the kids got by the moose with no trouble. Often, firing a shot near a moose will spook it, and it will run off. Many mushers also carry a flare gun when training in case they run into a moose that won't get off the trail. They fire it at the feet of the moose. It sounds like a shotgun going off, exploding almost like a small firework when it hits, hopefully scaring the moose.

When the race marshal arrived on the scene, the moose was standing away from the trail, minding his own business munching away on some willows. Sarah headed to the starting line with great anticipation, her dogs screaming with excitement. These dogs love to run and get excited every time we go on a training run, but they get super crazy at races. They know the difference, and it is certainly palpable. When Sarah took off, I was not sure who was more excited, Sarah or the dogs. They were really rolling, the two dogs matching stride-for-stride, gliding over the snow like their feet weren't even touching the ground, Sarah hanging on with her neck scarf flying straight behind her like a flag in a heavy wind. Then she was out of sight, and it seemed like forever before we saw her appear again, heading up the hill. The dogs were still running, looking so smooth that from the side, they looked like one dog. As she approached the finish line, I couldn't help but notice that the look of excitement that she had when she left the starting line had been replaced by a wide-eyed look of anxiety! She crossed the finish line, I grabbed her sled, and as we made our way back to the truck, all she could say was, "Moose!" She calmed down and told us she was having a great run and so much fun, but as she made the turn and started heading through the birch trees, she saw the moose on one side of the trail staring at the race marshal who was on the other side of the trail with his rifle pointed at the moose. Sarah didn't know what to do. Was she really going to have to go between them? The race marshal motioned for her to continue, and she did exactly that—she raced right between them. A brave little girl!

Sarah had another run-in with a moose a couple of years later, and this time, she had no backup; she was out there alone with her dogs. She was competing again in the Junior North American Championships. It was the third day of the race, and she was in third place, with not even a mile left when she came around a bend and encountered a moose standing in the middle of the trail! She slammed on her brake and stopped her team. The moose stood there, staring at her. Dogs raised or trained in Alaska would cower at the sight of a moose and would never provoke her (like my team did when I got stomped by the moose). But Sarah's team consisted of young dogs who were used to training at Bucks County Horse Park in Pennsylvania. Her dogs started barking like crazy at the moose. Did they think it was a horse? They didn't know enough to be scared. The moose just looked at them and moved off to the side. Sarah recognized her chance, so she called up her team and took off. The moose took off too and started running next to her, nostrils flaring, blowing snot out its nose. Sarah said she was so close she could have reached out and touched her. Finally, the moose turned off into the trees, and Sarah was safe. By the time she crossed the finish line, she couldn't say anything except, "Moose, moose, big moose!" She was able to hold onto third place even with an unscheduled stop for the moose. She had an amazing three days! The dogs were great, and the weather was perfect: sunny and in the mid-teens. Sarah was so excited with how the dogs ran and how they finished. Her excitement was a little dampened when she realized she would have to go up and give a speech at the Junior banquet, as was expected for all the top finishers. I thought this was a wonderful tradition and teaching moment for these young kids. Now a parent herself, with four little boys, we laugh about the wonderful times we had when Sarah was young, running dogs in Alaska.

*Sarah finishing a training run, coming down
the slough towards the cabin*

Most parents love to sit back and watch their kids do something they really enjoy. Youth sports can really help build confidence in children. Parents might be very nervous watching their children, whether it be on the soccer pitch, softball field, or any number of sports arenas. But if you really want to get that nervous feeling in the pit of your stomach, launch your kid into the Alaskan wilderness on a dog sled and see how *that* makes you feel! Many of our friends back in Pennsylvania could not believe we allowed Alex and Sarah to head off into the Alaskan bush alone behind a dog team. I would tell them honestly that I am more comfortable letting them head out into the Alaskan wilderness than allowing them to go to the mall as a young child. I can prepare them for anything they may encounter being alone in the woods, but the conversation about what they may encounter while in a busy mall is much more difficult and uncomfortable.

Sarah loved it when we had puppies, and she used to spoil them. She and her friends dressed them up in doll clothes and pushed them around in strollers—it used to drive me crazy. Mary Jo always said it was good for the puppies, and of course, the loving attention was, but these were my up-and-coming super stars, and they were wearing doll clothes! With both Sarah and Alex being so involved in raising our puppies, there was no doubt these human pups would grow up to be such well-adjusted adults. They could handle any situation as they had been exposed to a variety of life experiences.

When Sarah was twelve, she qualified for the International Federation of Sleddog Sports Junior World Championships that were taking place in Baqueira Beret, a small village in the Pyrenees mountains of Spain. We (Sarah and I) flew with her three-dog team out of JFK airport in New York. Again, we didn't give her the fastest or youngest dogs, but dogs that would listen to her and would not be afraid of the trip or the commotion surrounding a world championship with kids and dogs from all around the globe. The important thing here was not winning but for Sarah and the dogs to have a positive experience. Mary Jo and I recognized the rare opportunity for what it was. Who knew if this would ever happen again? When we were checking in at the airport, we had an adorable moment. When the ticketing agent leaned over the counter to say hello to Sarah's dogs, her lead dog, Heather, jumped up and put her front paws on the counter, looking very relaxed and almost human-like. I thought, *Well, she was a good choice.*

Sarah with Share and Me at the IFSS WC in Pla De Beret, Spain

We arrived in Barcelona as the sun was coming up over the Mediterranean Sea. It was beautiful, but it was also very warm and didn't feel like sled dog racing weather. The dogs were happy to get out of the plane. I had become friends with a sled dog racer from Portugal, and he had offered to pick us up at the airport and house our dogs in his truck during our stay. It was a four-hour drive up into the Pyrenees mountains, and we certainly found winter again as we climbed up the mountains. Sarah was excited but also very nervous. She was one of three American kids who made the trip, including a girl from Alaska and one from Minnesota. We checked into the hotel and rested. The next morning, we traveled to the race site to check in for the race, get her racing bib, and look at the trail.

It snowed every day of the three-day race, which made the trail hard to follow. Sarah didn't have the fastest team in the race, but she may have had the most experienced team there. All three dogs were at least seven years old. There was nothing that could have happened there that they hadn't seen at some point in their careers, and they knew how to follow and stay on the trail. Sarah said teams were running all over the place, going off the trail or stopping in the middle of it. Snowmobiles with TV cameramen filming the race would follow right behind the teams, and this was freaking out many dogs. Sarah said it was really chaotic, but her dogs ignored the commotion and just kept going. Sarah ended up winning the bronze medal for the United States! It was a wonderful trip and a great father-daughter experience.

That same season, Sarah competed in the Anchorage Fur Rendezvous Junior World Championship Sled Dog Race. The kids in this race go out in two-minute intervals, so every two minutes, a team leaves the starting chute. Faster teams end up catching and having to pass the slower teams. Your dogs must learn to run by other teams (and be passed) without getting distracted and wanting to play or, worse, wanting to fight. The most interesting aspect of that race took place before the race when another family severely underestimated us. Our dog truck at the time was really nice, and we fit right in; it looked like we belonged. That was the year we had driven up as a family. All of us were there getting Sarah ready to race, and we struck up a friendly conversation with a woman and her daughter, who were parked next to us. Her daughter drew the starting position one behind Sarah. The mom happened to walk behind our truck and noticed our license plate was from Pennsylvania. She asked me when we moved to Alaska, and when I said we didn't, her demeanor changed completely. She was no longer very nice. She took her daughter aside and started telling her how she was going to catch Sarah and would have to pass her. Then she came over to me to ask if our dogs are aggressive when they get passed. I told her I had no idea, as they had never been passed! She just assumed that if we were from Pennsylvania, we would obviously have no idea how to race sled dogs, and Sarah would be getting in her daughter's way. Sarah finished second, winning the silver medal and when she went up to get her trophy, I couldn't help but glance at the mother to see her embarrassed reaction.

In Fairbanks, at the Jeff Studdard tract (yes, they actually have designated sled dog trails in Alaska!), they groom the trail with a PistenBully groomer, a $300,000 machine complete with a Mercedes engine. The trail system in Fairbanks covers more than thirty miles. If you are out on a training run and miss a turn, it could be a long, cold, and dangerous ride, even without considering the wildlife you may encounter. The clubhouse is a large, hand-hewn log building set in a lovely meadow of fireweed. A beautiful wildflower, fireweed can grow as tall as six feet, with the top fourth covered in quarter-sized pink flowers. The meadow slopes down a gradual hill to a stand of birch trees that add to the color palette. During the summer, this is a lovely venue for weddings, and for years, they even had a Shakespeare theatre performing here in the meadow. In the winter, of course, it is all under a white blanket of snow, and the clubhouse serves more as a warming shed than a wedding venue.

Alex's junior musher career didn't involve run-ins with moose, but he had his own exciting moments. Two of the most serious incidents were caused by bad advice from his handler, who also happened to be his father (me). Like his sister, Alex started in the one-dog and then moved to the two-dog class. By the time Alex was ready to race in the three-dog class, Sarah was in high school and playing sports. She couldn't just take off for a few weeks and head to Alaska without majorly disrupting her school year. So Mary Jo began to stay home with Sarah, and just Alex would join me at the cabin with the dogs.

When Alex was going to compete in the three-dog Junior North American Championships, the first two days, he was to run the 5.9-mile trail, which he had never seen before. Both Mary Jo and Sarah thought it was a bad idea to have him run a trail he had never been around before. They were worried he could get lost or miss a turn. I wasn't worried as I was sending him out on the trail with Spirit and

Rodney in lead—two dogs who had been around that trail dozens of times and seemed very dependable. Spirit was the most reliable one—having her in lead was like driving a car. She would happily move to the right or left side of the trail if one side was better groomed than the other, simply if her musher spoke to her. She would also turn ninety degrees either way if asked. She liked Alex, so I knew she would listen to him. Rodney, on the other hand, just liked to run as fast as he could. Listening to the musher was not high on his priority list; it was almost like his musher was an unnecessary distraction! But he would listen to Spirit, and she could—and would—push him all over the trail. She truly was the boss bitch!

Alex just had to tell Spirit to turn right when he saw the sign for the 5.9-mile turn. I told him to slow them down when he saw that turn, as it was a ninety-degree turn. He would be traveling at least twenty miles per hour, and if he didn't slow the team down going into the turn, he would flip the sled for sure and possibly hit the trees that lined the turn. I told him that after he negotiated the turn, he could ease off the brake and let them go back to full speed, as the next turn back onto the main trail was gradual, and he could negotiate it at full speed.

When Alex left the starting chute, the dogs were strung out nicely. Alex was holding them back as the first half mile was a slight downhill, and he didn't want them going out too fast. (I have seen a few dogs get hurt going off the hill too quickly as overly excited mushers get caught up in the moment.) I felt proud watching this young kid handle his team so well. I thought, *Mary Jo and I have done a pretty good job teaching him about dogs.* After a couple of minutes, he disappeared from view as he entered into the forest, mostly white spruce, with some birch and poplar mixed in. I had started my watch when he left the chute so I could keep track of his time, and knowing how fast the dogs would be traveling, I had a good idea when he should be coming back into view as he climbed the hill back to the finish line. I started to get concerned as time passed. I had no idea what was happening out on the trail, but I did know something wasn't right because I should have heard him announced by this time.

Alex racing in the Junior North American
Championships, Fairbanks, AK
Photo credit: Dave Partee

The race organizers have an announcer who gives updates throughout the race on how the teams are progressing down the trail. They have radio contact with the halfway point, and they make an announcement, giving the bib number of the team and the running time. They say when each team had made the turn and were heading home towards the finish line. It was always a big relief when you heard your kid's name because you would know your kid had made the turn and was heading home. I knew something was wrong as I was timing Alex's team, and I knew exactly how long it would take him to get to that turn. But they were making no announcement! He was the first team out of the chute, which also became a concern as the first team on the trail would also be the one that could potentially run into moose, snowmobiles, or skiers. I kept looking at my watch, waiting and listening for some kind of announcement. I started to worry that he could have run into a moose. I can assure you my heart was in my throat.

Then, finally, over the loudspeaker, I heard something that I certainly did not expect: "Well, team number one has made the turn. Unfortunately, there is no driver with it!" My heart sank. *Where was Alex? Was he alright?* This honestly was worse than no news! Two race officials immediately jumped on snowmobiles and raced out on the incoming trail, looking for the loose team and the missing junior musher. I had sent him out on a trail he had never been around against the wishes of his mom and sister. I knew this was not going to play well back at our house in Sellersville, Pennsylvania.

The problem was I had not traveled the 5.9-mile trail for a long time, as most of my training involved the ten- or twelve-mile trail. I had forgotten that there is also a ninety-degree turn coming out of the turnaround! Alex did exactly what I told him to do and finally listened to me! He slowed them down going into the turn, then let them speed up so they were going way too fast, and he flipped when they hit the second ninety-degree turn. He hit the trees and lost the team! Amazingly, the only thing that was hurt was his pride. The dogs, however, never slowed down; they continued racing down the trail, heading for the finish line! Alex jumped up from the deep snow and started chasing the team, but they quickly disappeared around the next bend. One of his native friends, running the team that went out behind him, caught up to him running down the trail and stopped. Alex jumped on his sled, and they continued down the trail, looking for his runaway team.

The race officials on snowmobiles finally caught up with Alex's runaway dog team. They stopped the team, and one official stayed with the team while the other official continued looking for Alex. He soon found him safely heading down the trail on the sled with his friend. Alex was soon reunited with his team, got back on his sled, and continued to the finish line, where I was waiting with my heart racing and worrying about him and the team. Back at the truck, after we took care of the dogs, Alex just kept saying, "Dad, we were flying! I can't believe I lost the team; we were just flying. I can't believe I lost them!" A musher's worst nightmare is losing your dog team. After we took care of the dogs, we had to call Mom and Sarah. I sure didn't want to make that call. I let Alex talk first, and he was so excited about how well the dogs were running that he softened them up before I had to face the music.

The next year, Alex was preparing to run in the four-dog Junior North American Championship. He really wanted to win this race because when Sarah ran the four-dog class, she finished second. Like a participant in any typical sibling rivalry, he wanted to do better than his sister. When Sarah ran it, she got in a bad tangle, passing a team on the first day. She lost a good bit of time getting her dogs untangled from the other team and finished second for the day. She won on day two and day three but couldn't make up for what she lost on day one. Often, a bad draw can really affect how you finish. Alex was warned that his draw for the four-dog was not a good one as the team ahead of him was slow and had some unruly and nasty dogs in it. He would catch and have to pass them, and his friend told him to be ready. It was also very cold, about −20°F, but Alex had the best cold weather gear we owned, including big heavy fur mittens for warmth. Under the mittens were light gloves that would allow him to handle the dogs more easily. The mittens were attached to a knitted rope that went around your neck so you could take them off and let them hang at your sides. When you weren't using them, you just spun them a couple of times behind your back, and they were out of the way until you needed them. A lot of us had these as little kids so we wouldn't lose our mittens in the snow.

Alex had decided that when he caught the team ahead of him, he would lose too much time taking off his mitts and spinning them behind his back. But if you just let them hang at your side when working with the dogs, they often get tangled. He said he wanted to go out of the starting chute in his light gloves until his team had passed by the team in front of him, and then put his mitts on. He was worried if the other musher's dogs did jump into his team, it would waste time to remove his mitts. I couldn't argue with the logic, but as the adult in the room, I should have said, "No, Alex, wear your mitts."

The team that went out ahead of Alex really was pretty slow, and Alex just shot out of the chute. I had no doubt he would catch her right away. I started my watch and waited nervously. They announced that Alex had made the turn. Judging by the time on my watch, he must have been rolling. It was close to four minutes before they announced that the team ahead of Alex had made the turn, so he obviously passed her. Soon, I could see him break out of the trees and head up the hill towards the finish. But as he got closer, something looked a little strange. He was hunched over the sled, and as he came into the finishing chute, I saw that he still had only his light gloves on! His fingers were so frostbitten he was unable to hold the handlebar with them, so he clung on with his wrists over the handlebar. I got him back to the truck, and he asked me to help him with the dogs as he couldn't feel his hands—they were completely numb from the cold. It turned out that after he passed the team ahead of him, his mittens got knotted behind his back, and he was unable to get them loose. He had to run the whole trail with light gloves at −20°F. He said when he could, he rotated placing his hands one at a time in his parka pocket. But the trail has a lot of curves, and you need both hands on the handlebars. Still, Alex came in first place, and he was happy. As you can imagine, I was again dreading that call home. Alex was pretty excited to tell them about winning the heat. Mary Jo knew how cold it was going to be, and when she asked him how bad it was, he then told her about his hands. Mary Jo sure wasn't very happy with me! Alex went on to win day two and day three so he ended up winning the four-dog Junior North American Championship! We were so proud of him and his dogs.

Alex also qualified to represent the United States in the 2009 International Federation of Sleddog Sports Junior World Championship that took place in Daaquam, Quebec. Alex had three good runs and, like his sister, won a Bronze Medal. Alex was bummed as he lost to two kids from France who won Gold and Silver. He likes to tell people they flew over with a professional to wax their runners each day, but all he had was his dad to do his.

Alex with his bronze medal and proud family at the Daaquam, Quebec IFSS World Championships

Many of the families that have kids who grow up racing sled dogs believe it brings a different level of maturity than most other kids their age. These kids are out on the trail by themselves with their dogs without adults to help them. When they get into a situation, they have to figure it out on their own—the grown-ups aren't there to bail them out. They must make quick decisions on their own. Also, after every race, there are awards ceremonies, and the top finishers are expected to give a short acceptance speech, which can be difficult for many youngsters.

CHAPTER 20

◆

Mary Jo Runs the Anchorage Women's Fur Rendezvous

Mary Jo grew up in Mt. Airy, a historic neighborhood in Northwest Philadelphia. She really didn't know anything about sled dogs until we met at New Bolton Center during graduate school. Her family had a pet dog growing up, and as I mentioned, she really has a way with animals. During our sled dog racing careers, many of our friends would suggest that she is the better dog musher between the two of us. No doubt some of it was good-natured ribbing, giving me a hard time, but certainly, there was an element of truth in it. Honestly, it didn't bother me at all, and I would usually joke back, *"Well, she did learn from the best!"*

Mary Jo starting at the Limited North American Championship
Photo credit: Dave Partee

Mary Jo always has a calming influence on the dogs, which can really be an advantage in racing. I think I probably have a more competitive nature than she does, but the dogs we raised would run for either of us equally as well. Once in a while, we'd have a dog that performed better for one or the other of us. Jessie was certainly *my* dog; he just seemed to sense what I wanted. Mary Jo's dog was a little grey saddleback named Bow. That was her given name, as she came to us as a puppy, but she became Bow Bow among our family. She just loved Mary Jo and would do anything she asked. She had unlimited energy and excitement and raced competitively until she was ten. People who saw her in the starting chute at her retirement age would swear she was a yearling because of how crazy she was. She was Mary Jo's main leader for all those years. It was tough for Mary Jo when it was time to retire Bow Bow, as she relied on her leading up in front of her team. Bow Bow moved into training our puppies for the next few years and was just as happy running as a trainer.

Early on in Mary Jo's sled dog career, Bow showed just how intelligent and valuable she was. We were in the Upper Peninsula of Michigan near the Iron River on our way to races in Minnesota and Wisconsin. We had stopped at a friend's house and were planning to train on an abandoned railroad bed that he kept groomed for sled dogs. We had never been on the trail, but he said it was simple: straight out for a couple of miles, over a road crossing, another couple of miles, then a groomed turn he'd created in a field, then back home. Simple enough. I asked about the road crossing, but he said not to worry as it hadn't been plowed. He would go first, then Mary Jo would go with her team, and then I would hook up my team and follow in the back.

The idea was to have Mary Jo between us as she hadn't been running dogs that long. He went, then I launched Mary Jo, and I watched her team roll down the trail before I hooked my team and left. It was really beautiful running through a forest of balsam fir and white spruce. As the road crossing came into view, I got really worried as I could see Mary Jo jumping up and down, waving her arms, and there was no dog team! She lost them. As I got there, she was freaking out—the road had been plowed! She couldn't see this as she approached the road; she just saw the trail continuing to the other side and into the woods. She said before she could stop the dog team, they had already dropped off the snowbank nearly three feet down onto the plowed road. She could get the dogs to turn right or left, but she couldn't get them to go straight because they had a three-foot snowbank in front of them. She couldn't just let them run down the plowed road in either direction because, on a plowed road, you have no control, no brake, no snow hook, and there is the possibility of cars or trucks on the road. They couldn't see the trail on the other side. She had Bow Bow in lead with a big young dog, Ranger, who was in training to be a leader, and four young dogs behind them. She said the young dogs just finally got too excited and bolted to the right. Mary Jo got flipped into the air and came down, smacking her head on the road, and she lost the team.

We spun my team around to head back to the truck and to start driving the roads, looking for the loose team. She jumped on the back of the runners behind me, and off we went, heading back to the truck. You never want to lose a dog team as anything can happen to them without you, but losing them on a plowed road really increases the danger. I felt awful for Mary Jo as I knew she was beating herself up. I was also mad at myself for sending her out there and putting her in that situation. The dogs were last seen running down a plowed road, but we didn't even know the name of the road! It seemed like it took forever to get back to the truck, and when we did, quite a surprise awaited us. There was Bow Bow and the whole dog team standing at the truck, waiting for a treat and some water like they have countless other times after a run. The sled wasn't even turned over! I never considered that they would find their way back to the truck! Mary Jo started crying and hugging Bow Bow. I stood there dumbfounded.

Soon, our friend arrived back at the truck with his dog team, and he was really worried as well, as he hadn't seen either one of us. He said the plow came down the road after he crossed but before Mary Jo got there. He felt horrible. Then we told him about Mary Jo's team. He said when they went down the right side of the road, they must have turned right when they got to the first intersection. Another right turn at the following intersection would have brought them back to the truck! It is amazing to me that a dog who had never been there before knew how to find her way home. Without Bow's leadership, it could have been such a disaster. Usually, a dog team likes to just run straight; they are not big on making turns because they are just racing each other.

Mary Jo with Bow and Ranger, her lead dogs

One of the most interesting races Mary Jo competed in was the 1999 Anchorage Fur Rendezvous Women's World Championship Sled Dog Race. Mary Jo was a rookie in the race, which that year boasted the biggest field ever to compete in the event and included women from Sweden, Germany, Canada, and the United States, including Iditarod royalty Susan Butcher and Dee Dee Jonrowe. These two amazing women really love and have the innate ability to work with dogs. They decided to try sprint racing as a change of pace from the Iditarod, a distance race most people are more familiar with. I first met Susan when we were both speaking at a sled dog conference in Germany. Susan was aware of my work in nutrition but not necessarily my background in sled dog sports. When I was introduced to her, and they told her I was a dog musher from Pennsylvania, she just smiled and said, "There is no such thing." Over the years, we became good friends with her and her husband, David Monson. Later, as she transitioned out of the sport, our conversations went from raising dogs to raising kids. Sadly, Susan passed away in 2006.

At the Women's Rendezvous, Mary Jo was going to run a team of twelve dogs, and I was going to be her handler, which was a bit of a switch as I usually raced the main team. My lack of experience as a handler—or maybe lack of focus—sadly would become very apparent to the entire field on the first day. On the bottom of the runners of our sleds is an aluminum channel over which you slide plastic runners, and at the very top, there is a small bolt that fastens the plastic to the aluminum channel so it can't slide off. The plastic runners came in different densities for different snow conditions. We also wax the plastic runners just like you would a pair of skis. I waxed three sets of runners to try the morning of the race, taking about ninety minutes per set. We got to the race site the first morning, and as you can imagine, Mary Jo was nervous. In Anchorage, the Alaskan Sled Dog and Racing Club (established in 1949) maintains the Tozier Track, which is a twenty-mile trail system that starts and ends at a ten-acre trailhead owned by the club. The parking area for mushers is a large semicircle with heavy posts sticking out of the ground at each parking spot to hook your dog team to, all aiming at the starting chute about twenty-five yards away. This field was stacked, so many teams could win this event, and it wouldn't have been a surprise. Mary Jo was also nervous as this was the biggest team she ever competed with. I tried to reassure her that both she and the dogs had been around the trail already, so they knew where they were going. I felt my words were falling on deaf ears as I was nervous as well. Why should she be calm?

I got the sleds down off the top of the truck and let the dogs out for a little drink. I tried the first set of runners, and they were pretty good. I would slide the runners on the aluminum channels and then give the sled a slight push across the packed snow, which I hoped was the same texture as the dog trail. Then I would just watch to see how it glided, stand on one runner, and give it a little push to see how easily it slides on the snow. The second pair was certainly better, but the third pair was amazing; it was a home run! That sled just kept going and going. I wasn't the only one that noticed. A couple of spots away, Susan saw it as well and said, "Oh my God, let me try it!" Before I knew it, there were about half a dozen people clamoring around my sled, asking all kinds of questions about the wax, the plastic, and so forth.

Finally, it was time to hook up the team and head to the starting chute. Mary Jo would be running Share and Ten in lead, two dogs with only one thing in common: they were both females. Share had brown eyes and was a medium size dog, about fifty-two pounds, black with a brown mask and underbelly. She was a happy-go-lucky dog that felt no pressure; whether she was in lead or back in the team, she just loved to run. She did have attention issues and a wandering eye, though. Anything along the trail could distract her: a squirrel, a bird, you name it. She never left the trail to chase anything, but sometimes, she made me worry. Ten was a perfect partner for her as she was all business. Share was happy to do whatever Ten wanted. Ten was a little smaller, all red, with brown eyes, really a beautiful dog. I always thought "Ten" was a great name for her; to me, she really was a "Perfect Ten."

We arrived at the starting line, and I kissed Mary Jo and told her to just have some fun. I had complete faith in her. The dogs were ready, and they took off down the trail. Everyone was in stride; it was beautiful to watch. The race had live radio coverage, so they were giving out checkpoint times (radio coverage also meant if there were any moose on the trail, you would get a warning about where you might encounter them). Starting positions were determined by a random draw, with teams leaving at two-minute intervals. All the rookies in the field would draw together and would go out after the veteran teams. The disadvantage of going out at the end of the pack is the trail might get a little chewed up from all the dogs that have been over it. The advantage is (if they have radio coverage and you are listening to it on headphones) you will hear the checkpoint time of your competitors before you get there, so you will know how you are doing. But you must remember to run your own race and focus on your dogs. You can't get caught up in what others are doing. Mary Jo didn't want to wear headphones, and she didn't care what others were doing. Her focus was her twelve dogs.

The checkpoint times were coming in, and I was so excited to hear that Mary Jo was doing incredibly well. She was holding her own against the best teams in the world, and her checkpoint times were in the top five. Just after the halfway point, things started to change. Her checkpoint times started to slow down, and she was falling behind. It got worse the closer she got to the finish line. I started to worry. *Did she go out too quickly? Had she taken too much out of the team early in the race so they were unable to finish strong?* That wasn't Mary Jo; no race was as important as the health and happiness of her dogs, she wouldn't push them. Besides, she wasn't listening to checkpoint times anyway, so she wouldn't get caught up in how well they were doing. Finally, Mary Jo crossed the finish line, and the dogs all looked good.

We got back to the truck, took their harnesses off, and gave them their Annamaet Glycocharge, a canine sports drink we designed to aid in the replenishment of muscle glycogen stores following exercise. They all eagerly drank and were bouncing around and happy; they didn't look like a dog team that would wear out on the back half of a race. After we took care of the dogs and put them away, I asked Mary Jo how the race had gone. She told me that in the first half of the race, the dogs were just rolling, and she was even trying to hold them back a bit. But she said after the halfway point, they just slowed down; the sled wasn't gliding like in the beginning, and then it started to make a bit of noise, like a squeaking sound. That made no sense to me as I had the wax spot on, and although it may have worn off in twelve miles, she shouldn't have slowed down like that.

As Mary Jo wrapped up the lines and harnesses, I picked up the sled and put it on the roof of the dog truck. As I slid it up on the truck, I saw nothing but aluminum rails! The plastic runners I'd spent so much time waxing were gone! Now it made sense: Mary Jo was having a wonderful run until the runners came off. She didn't notice she lost her runners as she was focusing on the dogs in her team. I quickly realized what had happened: early that morning, I was checking to see which runners had the best wax, and I found the best set. During the commotion that followed when everyone came over to see how great these runners were, I forgot to put the bolts through the plastic runners and into the aluminum rails. This was totally my fault; I was horrified, embarrassed, and incredibly pissed off at myself. A handler's worst nightmare: should I tell her? Well, that was an easy answer but a difficult discussion! I have to admit, my first thought was that maybe Mary Jo wouldn't need to hear about this. But we have always been honest with each other, so reluctant as I was, I had to tell her I had ruined her race. She had such a good run going, but she certainly couldn't make up that time, especially against that field. She ended up finishing twenty-first out of twenty-five on the first day.

I swallowed my pride and called her over to show her the sled with no plastic runners. To her credit, she didn't get mad; she just chuckled and said, "Well, that explains a lot!" Being a wonderful wife and my best friend, she took it in stride. "We still have two more days!" she said. That evening, there was a knock at our hotel room door, and once again, I learned why honesty is the best policy. Our close friends, Lloyd and Kathy, came into our room carrying a set of runners to see if we knew who may have lost them during the race. Lloyd took one look at my face and knew exactly whose runners they were! I said something like, "I was wondering where I left those," followed by a nervous laugh! I was busted; I knew I would never live this down.

As it turned out, after the first heat was completed earlier in the day, Lloyd and Kathy had decided to train some of their dogs that hadn't raced earlier. They ran a double sled, which is when you hook up two sleds, one behind the other, each with a driver. Just before they reached the halfway point, they saw a runner lying on the edge of the trail, and Lloyd scooped it up. They went another mile or so, and there was the next one. When they got to their truck and were talking while putting away their dogs, they realized Mary Jo was the last team out of the chute, and they were the first team to train after the race, so they figured they were probably her runners. They also realized this would be the fault of her race handler, me! The next morning, everyone gave me a hard time about making sure her runners were bolted on properly. Even when we got into the starting chute, the sled holders who helped control your team—who I didn't even know—

were hollering, "*Runner check!*" and someone would check the bolts. Everyone was having fun busting my chops. They needled me for years about not bolting on our runners! After three days of racing, Kathy won the race, and Mary Jo was able to climb back into the money. She did an amazing job coming back in the race; I was so proud of her and the dogs.

Around this time, Lloyd took to calling me *Black Cloud Downey* because of all the bad luck I seemed to have. He was a master at pulling my chain and giving me a hard time. If something could go wrong in a situation, he was convinced it would happen to me. But I never saw it that way; I always thought there was a silver lining that would appear and make it all better. Things always worked out the best for me. This book is filled with stories like that—some humorous, some scary, and some self-inflicted.

Mary Jo has had a wonderful career racing sled dogs, and she truly enjoyed it. She won an IFSS World Cup Gold Medal and won several races in Minnesota and Wisconsin, as well as Alaska. She barely missed a Bronze Medal at the IFSS World Championship in Fairbanks, Alaska. Racing really became a family activity that we all enjoyed, and it bonded us. It is a labor-intensive activity, but like they always say, if you really enjoy it, it isn't work.

CHAPTER 21

◆

Tales from the Trail

Alaska is an amazing place—vast and beautiful. People may not realize how big it is. Everyone thinks Texas is big, but you can fit Texas into Alaska twice. The state is bigger than Texas, California, and Montana combined! In addition to the size, I am always amazed that the difference between the low and the high temperatures in the state is often over 100 degrees during the winter! Here is a bit of Alaska trivia for you: Alaska is obviously the most western state in the United States. Did you know that Alaska is also the easternmost state in the United States? The Aleutian Islands cross longitude 180°, so Alaska can be considered the easternmost state as well as the westernmost.

People hear me talk about our wildlife encounters when we are out running a team of dogs. I often get asked if I have ever run into a bear on the trail. When we are in Alaska, from December to March, most bears are hibernating, so that isn't an issue. If you do see a bear during that time of year, however, that is a great cause for concern. It is extremely rare, but a bear that is awake during the winter is often referred to as a "sour bear." It may be awake because of starvation or gut issues that have awakened it during hibernation. These bears have been known to be very dangerous. In our twenty Alaskan winters, I only remember hearing about one bear sighting, and that was down more towards Anchorage.

As I have mentioned, we spent twenty winters in the interior of Alaska. The days get short during the winter, so we spent most of our time outside with a headlamp on so we could see to do our chores. Sunrise to sunset on the shortest day of the year is only ninety minutes. We timed training so we would be on the trail running our dog teams during the light. Most often, this meant watering the dogs in the dark in the morning and then feeding them in the dark after a run. I read somewhere once that "A true Alaskan carries two flashlights with them from the middle of September until May. One for everyday use and another to loan to the person who does not adhere to this!"

To me, one of the most amazing parts of Alaska is the Aurora Borealis, more commonly known as the northern lights. It is a most spectacular display in the night sky. The lights dance across the sky in a slow waltz, and they change colors as well. Most common is a neon green but sometimes pink appears, and when they are really strong, they might also be red, violet, and white. I found them mesmerizing. Sometimes, later at night, after tending to the dogs for the last time or after returning from grooming the dog trail, I would see them dancing in the sky. I would just lay back in the snow with my head resting on a snowbank and stare at the sky, watching them. These moments were relaxing, de-stressing, and truly good for the soul. I used to tell people I could hear them as well, and they would usually laugh at me. But recently, scientists did a study and found that about 5 percent of the really strong Aurora Borealis do make noise, typically a crackling or a whooshing sound. I only ever heard the crackling, and it wasn't often, but I feel vindicated that it has since been proven that they can make noise.

People travel from all over the world to see the northern lights, and there are a couple of interesting myths regarding them. In Japanese folklore, if a woman becomes pregnant under the northern lights, her child will be blessed with good luck and fortune. A friend who had a small bed-and-breakfast had some foreign tourists staying with him, and at dinner, they asked, "When do they turn on the northern lights?" Mary Jo and I did see them in Pennsylvania one time, but they were not very bright and did not have much color. In fact, if you didn't know what you were looking for, you might not have seen them. The local weather person in our area said they may be visible, so we were watching for them. These lights are just one of the many wonderful side benefits of our time spent training and racing our dog teams in Alaska.

As you have read, moose encounters on the training trails in Alaska aren't that frequent, but they are often memorable. Most are non-threatening, especially if you see them in time because you can stop and wait for them to clear the trail—which they are encouraged to do by an excited barking dog team. But occasionally, you will run into a moose who takes exception to you interrupting their dinner. The colder and harder the winter, the more irritable the moose population is, and the more likely the second of these scenarios will be.

One time, Mary Jo and I were out double sledding. This helps keep the speed down for a slower training pace, which is sometimes needed because if you continually run dogs at race speeds in training, they will eventually wear down. Using two sleds also gives you two brakes and two sets of snow hooks, which allows for better control, which is especially helpful when training bigger teams with more power. This day, we were training a sixteen-dog team, so our leaders, Vinnie and Veto, ran more than seventy feet in front of the sleds. We were training at the Jeff Studdard track in Fairbanks, out for a nice sixteen-mile run. About halfway through the run, we were coming around a sweeping turn to the right through a beautiful large group of aspens when I saw a moose off to the left. Instead of turning away from us, I saw her hackles go up, her ears go down, her head lower, and she started to charge the team from the side. I hollered, "Here she comes!" Then I screamed at the dogs for more speed, hoping we could get around the curve before she got to us. I could see that the dogs and I would make it, but Mary Jo was on the back sled, and the moose looked like she was zeroed in on her. I could not look back as we were heading around a curve, and if I took my focus off riding the sled and tipped over, we would lose momentum, and for sure, the moose would be on us. I focused on trying to get us all around the curve and hoped for the best.

Afterward, Mary Jo said the moose was bearing down on her, and all she could see was snot coming out of the moose's nose and the whites of her eyes. She thought, *Oh no, here it comes!* She closed her eyes and waited for the impact. . . but nothing happened! The moose had charged the team, but when it got there, it just stopped and let her go! We were both shaken but safe. Neither of us spoke for a while, just taking in everything that had just happened. Realizing how lucky we were and very much relieved, I couldn't help myself, and I hollered back at Mary Jo, "I had my knife out and was going to cut you loose. I figured there was no sense in both of us getting hurt!" I couldn't help but add a bit of levity to a stressful situation, something I have done many times in my life. Mary Jo didn't quite see the humor as I did, but I wasn't the one who had a moose bearing down on me.

I have competed in more than three hundred sled dog races in my career, with most of them taking place in the lower forty-eight states and Canada. The ones I have the best memories of tend to be the bigger races I have won. Many races have faded from memory, but others I remember not because of how I finished but because of something that may have happened during the event. One such race was the Festival du Voyageur in Winnipeg, Manitoba—the biggest winter carnival in Western Canada at the time. For several years, they hosted a large sled dog race as part of the festival. It was such a nice venue that one year, it was chosen to host the International Federation of Sleddog Sports World Championships. I was honored to be selected to represent the United States at that event, one of four such times I was named to represent our country. I met some wonderful mushers from all around the world at these world championships. I came home with some wonderful memories, but unfortunately no medals.

This particular year, the race organizers decided to make it more exciting for race fans, and they chose to have dual starts. This means two teams would be leaving the starting chute at the same time, side by side. This was not only exciting for race fans; it was also exciting for the driver and the dogs. It provided an additional challenge because it was hard to get separation from the team next to you. You really had to just forget about them and run your race. If you pushed your team to pull away from the other team too early, you risked tiring the team out and may have a hard time finishing strong. I was wary of the dual starts going into the race that year. Our main race leaders that year, Diane and Hooter, were very fast but young and inexperienced. I wasn't sure how they would react when they had to take off with a team next to them. They had never raced this way before. Hooter was an all-black, long and leggy female. Diane was the biggest female in our yard, mostly black with some white on her face and underbelly with blue eyes. She was just crazy to run and was all attitude. Relying on Hooter to be the brains of the outfit that day was scary. I wasn't sure they would always go the way I wanted, but I knew whatever way we went, we would be going very fast.

*Diane, with an intense stare that belied a
happy personality and a crazy attitude*

The race site was in a park on the edge of town. After leaving the starting chute, your team ran about three hundred yards, made a sharp left, and ran down a long steep bank where you made another left onto the Assiniboine River. You would head down the river about five miles, loop around to the other side, and head back up the river, making your way back up the bank and into the park. They had a mushers meeting the night before the race, where officials reviewed the trail and handed out the starting order. I would be going out next to a Quebecer musher who was a friend. However, I knew he took racing seriously and would be out to win. The other problem was our teams were comparable, so it would be difficult for either of us to get away from the other. Having that constant competition close by can also wear out your dog team mentally.

On race day, the temperature was in the mid-20°s, so not too cold. I was wearing Gore-Tex wind pants over long underwear. My insulated jacket only reached to about my beltline. I thought it wasn't cold enough for my parka or insulated anorak, both of which reached mid-thigh. This is a mistake I never made again!

With two teams side-by-side in the starting chute, ready to race, the noise was deafening! We took off like a rocket! By the time we had traveled the three hundred yards to the turn, we were already almost one full team length ahead. As my dogs started going around the turn to head down to the river, my competitor's lead dogs were right next to my sled. I was worried, as I went around the corner, that my sled would hit his leaders. As I was making the turn, I tried to move my sled over to avert hitting his dogs. I knew my competitor wasn't going to slow them down to avoid my sled. Trying to move my sled over as I was going around a tight corner and down a steep bank was a big mistake. I flipped; my sled went up in the air and came down on its side with me still hanging on the handlebar. I slid down the long embankment on my face, hanging on for dear life. There was no stopping my team, especially as the team next to us had started to pass me, as my speed had slowed down some while I was dragging. Now I had another problem. The trail down the long embankment to the river had really gotten chewed up by mushers trying to hold back their teams, either riding their brakes or standing on a drag mat trying to slow them down. The loose snow was deep as we descended the hill. Well, my jacket wasn't long enough, and the snow started to fill my pants as I was dragged down the hill. By the time we got to the bottom, enough snow had gotten into my pants that they were literally peeled down to my knees! The dogs made the turn onto the river, hot in pursuit of the team we went out next to, which was gradually pulling away as my sled was still on its side, and I was dragging down the trail on my stomach, trying to hold on. We didn't have the best snow cover on the river either; the trail had about a two-inch hard pack on top. Off the sides of the trail, the loose snow was about six inches deep. My arms were really wearing out. I didn't know how long I could hold on. I just knew I couldn't let go! Losing the team on the river could be a disaster. The trail was so fast if the team lost the resistance on the sled that I, the musher, provided, a dog could really get hurt or worse!

I had to do something. I was starting to lose my grip on the sled; my legs, especially my knees, were getting chewed up by the trail. I finally reached into the sled with one arm and grabbed the snow hook. I was afraid to just press it into the trail as I didn't think it would catch and stop me. So I kicked my right leg out into the soft snow along the trail, and that pulled the sled over to the edge. Then I pushed the snow hook into the soft snow with all the strength I had left! It sank into the snow and caught on the ice enough to stop the dog team, but I didn't think it would hold for long. I quickly jumped up and flipped the sled back on its runners. The hook then popped, and off we went, but at least both the sled and I were upright! I grabbed for the snow hook bouncing along the sled before it got wrapped around the runners. I got it put away, and then I started trying to get the snow out of my pants and pull them back up. I thank God this was before cell phones, as I can't imagine the pictures or video of me being dragged down the river in the middle of Winnipeg in my long underwear—that would be quite embarrassing!

After that, the rest of the run went smoothly. That was a painful night for me; both my knees were swollen and had brush burns on them, as did my thighs. My friends and Mary Jo suggested that I scratch and not run day two, as we were out of contention, but I decided to see how I felt in the morning. Mary Jo and I were going to be heading from Winnipeg to Alaska the morning after the race, and the dogs would be off for a few days for the drive. I planned to use the next day's heat as basically a training run, just let the dogs go out and have fun.

The next morning, I was still sore but decided I could stand on the sled for the run. Off we went, Hooter and Diane doing a great job. We got the jump on the team next to us and pulled away from them. Then, we caught and passed the two teams that went two minutes ahead of us, and we even passed one of the teams that went out four minutes ahead of us. We were really rolling! We were heading back up the river towards home, and all that was left was to make the hard left-hand turn to head up the bank off the river and into the park. At the last second, Diane made a hard right instead of going left and wrapped us around some straw bales that were blocking the trail to prevent teams from going back down the river. It caught both me and Hooter completely by surprise. Hooter had no chance to react— Diane pulled her right in! The whole team was tangled, and it took me forever to get everyone straightened out and back on the right trail. All that time we had gained, we gave back. The only explanation I can imagine is Diane didn't want to end the run; she wanted to keep running! It was a simple choice: go left and go home, go right and go back out on the river. I guess she wanted to keep going.

We ended up in last place and got the "Red Lantern Award," which was given to the last-place team. I think that is the only one I ever got (If I did get any other Red Lantern awards, I've blocked them from my memory!). I learned two things at that race: first, Diane was a good sled dog, but she needed a lot more training as a lead dog; second, never ever wear a short coat while racing. I was determined to come back and redeem myself, and I did. The next year, I won the Festival du Voyageur Sled Dog Race.

CHAPTER 22

❖

The End of an Era

I knew our racing career was coming to an end after I achieved my goal of winning the Limited North American Championship in Fairbanks, Alaska. Mary Jo and I knew we couldn't keep doing this forever. As the kids got older, it was harder and harder for them to leave school in Pennsylvania and live in Alaska for the winter. Once they got to high school and were involved in sports, it just didn't work anymore. If they couldn't come to Alaska, then neither could Mary Jo, as someone needed to be in Pennsylvania for them. The last year I raced, I spent the winter in the cabin by myself. It was tough.

It was also time for our dogs to retire. Mary Jo and I had also been thinking about what this day would mean for us and our dogs because they were like our kids. We knew once we stopped racing, we weren't going to get rid of any of the dogs. They were such a big part of our lives. We made the difficult decision to stop raising puppies because when we stopped racing and training our sled dogs, we didn't want to have a bunch of young dogs who would be living out their prime years being bored. Our plan was to keep running the dogs as long as they enjoyed it, even if they wouldn't be racing. We trusted our instincts to know when it was time to stop. We stopped racing when the dogs were all over nine years old. This may be old by most standards, but our dogs had been well-fed and well-cared for all their lives. (Some people who know us would say *pampered*, but no doubt this is further proof of how a great diet and good exercise will allow for a long, enjoyable life, whether two-legged or four-legged!)

While I enjoyed all those years training in the Pine Barrens, it wasn't an easy trek for me: it was a seventy-five-mile drive each way from my home, taking both the Pennsylvania Turnpike and the New Jersey Turnpike. It got expensive, with tolls and diesel fuel costs. Southern New Jersey can get very warm as well, so I had to get there as the sun was coming up. I would wake up around 3:30 or 4:00 in the morning, load the dogs into the truck, and drive about two hours to our training area. Then, another two-hour drive home after training. The trails are so nice; it was worth it while we were racing.

I would occasionally be stopped by other rangers who were unaware that their supervisor had given me permission to train with my ATV as long as I wasn't running the motor. But early one Sunday morning, a young ranger was a little over the top. As I turned off the main road onto the forest service road in my truck full of dogs, pulling a trailer with the ATV on it, a ranger turned in behind me and followed me for a bit before turning on his flashing lights and his siren. I pulled over, and then he went by me and turned his truck, angling in front of mine, to block me in. I guess he did this, so I couldn't drive off. Then he got out of his truck, and as he started walking back to me, he unbuckled his gun! I thought, *You must be kidding me!* He walked up to me with his hand on his pistol, still in its holster. He barked out, "What are you doing here?"

"I am just going to train my dogs," I answered.

"Not on that you are not!" he shouted as he pointed to the ATV.

"I have permission from your supervisor," I said.

"We'll see about that!" He took out his radio and called the supervisor, and I could hear the conversation over his radio. I heard the supervisor tell him that I had been doing that for years and I was not hurting anything. I was not running the motor, and he should just leave me alone. He was obviously annoyed with the response. I watched his shoulders slump as he buckled his gun, walked back to his truck, and took off. I waited until he was gone before I laughed.

Sadly, years later, it all came to an end one day in 2010 when another young ranger came up to my truck and asked what I was doing there. When I gave her the same explanation about training my dogs on my ATV and doing it for years with the supervisor's permission, she said, "I have bad news for you. We have a new supervisor, and he is an absolute prick!" I was amazed that she would say that to me, someone she had never seen or met before in her life. I realized this guy must be a real jerk. She told me if the previous supervisor had given me permission, this guy would deny it because he hated him so much. She said I could train that day, but I couldn't come back. This was a shocker for me and very disappointing, but it was a conversation I knew would happen at some point. Something amazing happened as I was driving out of the forest service lane towards the highway that day. I looked up and a bald eagle was flying along with me up in the sky. I took this as a sign. This was back when bald eagles were very rare in New Jersey. Bald eagles are highly revered and considered sacred by Alaska Natives. Seeing that bald eagle really had a calming effect on me. I knew then it was going to be alright; it was okay to say goodbye to a place that had been so important to me for so many years. The New Jersey Pine Barrens will always hold a special place in my heart.

December 24, 2010—Christmas Eve—was the last time I hooked up our dog team for a run. Honestly, it made for a weird holiday season. On one hand, it was nice just to relax and enjoy family and the festivities. On the other hand, it was a weird feeling; for practically the last forty years, I have always been thinking about heading out with the dogs to go training or racing somewhere. For the longest time, I would wake up at 3:30 a.m. and think, *Time to go train the dogs*! As we celebrated New Year's Eve that year, I will always remember what Mary Jo said to me: "Your life isn't over; we have just closed one chapter of our lives and are starting a new one!" She was so right. The dogs weren't the only ones getting a little long in the tooth; I was getting old as well.

Many times, toward the end of my career, I chuckled to myself, thinking of the advice my friend Harvey gave me when he retired from the sport. He said, *"You wait until you get older; there will be a point where it is hard to snap a dog into the lines. Your hands just don't work so well, and your hand-eye coordination isn't what it once was."* Was he ever right! Trying to put a snap on the harness of a crazy excited sled dog got harder and harder.

We hadn't built a dog barn in Pennsylvania because the dogs were always in Alaska in the winter when it was cold. After we stopped going to Alaska, the dogs were obviously getting older, and we decided they missed having a dog barn. It was time to build one here at home. The cold gets to us more as we age, and dogs are the same. Although not a log building, the barn we built in Pennsylvania is insulated and has tongue and groove pine on the inside to give us that Alaskan feel. It even has a small loft. It is heated in the winter and has four windows with screens and a ceiling fan for the summer. The barn sits in the middle of a large fenced-in area, so the dogs could run free and have plenty of shade as they played amongst the large maple, hickory, and ash trees. Beyond the fence is a thousand-acre state parcel of game lands that further adds to the quiet serenity. It is truly a cabin in the woods. Our sled dogs were a big pack, and like any group of individuals, they didn't always see eye to eye, but for the most part, they were a happy bunch. The dogs loved this barn just like they did in Alaska.

As I mentioned, we stopped racing when the youngest dogs were about nine years old. We had lost our training grounds in the Pine Barrens, but we still had the wheel. We continued letting them run on the wheel for a few more years until it became obvious it was getting hard for them. Even after that, they enjoyed hanging out in the woods surrounding the dog barn. It was tough as the dogs aged, and eventually, they started to pass away one by one. It never gets easy to lose a dog. We knew this day was coming and felt blessed that they lived long and healthy lives, many reaching sixteen years old before passing. The dog barn was there for them to hang out in; they were always protected from the rain or snow. These were not house dogs. Bringing them into the house made them uncomfortable and led to excessive panting and pacing, always looking to escape back outside. But they loved the dog barn with its familiar smells. We didn't keep it as warm as our house, a temperature they would most likely describe as hot.

For many years, when one of our dogs died, we had them cremated. Sadly, over time, we collected a lot of urns. Some people find this a little disturbing, especially when I tell them that in the walk-in closet of our bedroom, the entire length of one shelf was covered in urns. Mary Jo and I always thought that maybe we would take them to Alaska and spread their ashes on the trails they ran on. We couldn't keep their ashes in the house forever as the dogs never liked coming into the house to begin with! A couple of years ago, we came up with a better idea. With the tractor, I leveled the ground and built a rock wall around three sides of the area where the large puppy pens used to be. Most of the dogs were born and raised there. Just as the snow began to fall—in a snowfall expected to be from four to six inches deep—Mary Jo and I went out and spread all their ashes. We wanted the snow to blanket and hold them in place. It was a tough afternoon for us; we both got emotional. In a strange way, it felt good as well; it was almost like we were setting them free. In the spring, I went out and spread additional topsoil, and we planted wildflowers throughout the whole area. Now, every summer, we enjoy this beautiful wildflower garden and think about the dogs that made such an indelible mark in our hearts. As a beautiful consequence of the wildflowers growing there, the garden is alive with butterflies in the summer. When the dogs were alive, they would go crazy chasing butterflies—they got way more excited to chase a butterfly than a deer or even a cat.

One of the toughest decisions pet owners must face comes at the end of our older pets' lives. Often, there is a fine line between keeping them alive because of your love for them and your decision to do what is right for them and ease their suffering. That decision was really driven home by my favorite dog, Salt, who was in failing health at nineteen years old. A close friend of mine, a veterinarian, said to me, "*You know, you are being selfish keeping her alive. It is time.*" He was right, but it takes a special friend who can say that to you.

CHAPTER 23

There is Life After Racing

Though our sled dog racing days ended, our family continued another dog sport. Dock Diving first appeared in 1997 at the Incredible Dog Challenge and really took off after appearing on ESPN in 2000 Great Outdoor Games. Now, you can find dock diving events all over the country. I watched these events on TV, and it was great to see how excited the dogs were to fly through the air and splash down in the pool. Some of the best dogs jump more than thirty feet! The docks are typically 40 feet long, 7.5 feet wide, and about 2 feet above the water. Basically, you have your dog sit/stay at the far end of the dock while you walk to the other end of the dock at the water's edge. You release your dog, and they come racing along the length of the dock as you throw a bumper or toy over the water, and your dog leaps after it. It is similar to a long jump in the Olympics: the dog that jumps the farthest wins.

While I had enjoyed watching it, I really had no interest in participating in the sport. Then along came Kai, an amazing Australian Cattle Dog puppy that Sarah and her husband, Mike, got. Both Sarah and Alex had been looking for a dog, and both wanted Australian Cattle Dogs, also referred to as blue or red heelers, depending on color. Years ago, they had gotten a heeler for my birthday that we named Jessie (another Jessie!). Jessie was my constant companion—he went everywhere with me. Jessie took over for Mic as copilot on my trips to Alaska. He was a great dog, but he was no Mic; he wanted no part of herding bison off the road. Jessie's spirit lives on with his picture gracing the front of our Annamaet Lean Dog Food bag. Our friends who knew Jessie got a kick out of him being the poster boy on a product for obese dogs, as Jessie had a weight issue himself. Anyway, Alex and his girlfriend Madison, now his lovely wife, flew to Texarkana, Arkansas, to pick out a couple of puppies after Jessie passed. They came home with Kai for Mike and Sarah and his littermate, Kona, for himself.

Anyone who knows Australian Cattle Dogs understands they do best when they have a job or activity. If you don't give them a job, they may create one on their own, herding your kids or cats. Or keeping your yard clear of groundhogs and squirrels! They can be strong-willed, and many have an incredible herding drive. A more familiar herding breed is Border Collies, who often herd sheep by simply lowering their head and staring at their subject until they move. A Border Collie's handler provides guidance with a shrill whistle. An Australian Cattle Dog is a heeler, a name that comes from the way they move cattle by biting them in the heels. So, think about it—here is a breed that was genetically developed to bully an animal forty times its size. Do you really think you are going to intimidate them? They can take over a household if not properly handled, which may be why so many of them end up in shelters. They are amazingly intelligent and loyal companions, but they are not for everyone. We have now had at least one heeler in the house for over thirty years.

Kai is different than any other cattle dog we have had; he is obsessed with water. We can't keep him out of our pool. It was cute when he was a little puppy, but when he got older and he was staying with us, we would let him outside at night before we went to bed, and he would immediately go jump in the pool and swim around—then we had to deal with this soaking wet dog at bedtime. All he wants you to do is to throw something so he can bring it back to you; he won't leave you alone outside. In the middle of the summer, it is just too hot to be throwing a Frisbee or ball for him. So, I simply started to combine his two loves. I would throw the ball in the pool, and he would fly through the air to get it, splashing down and cooling off in the water. Sarah and Mike have four little boys, and they have done an amazing job with Kai's early training. He knows many commands, and he adores the boys, even if he is a little hard on their toys (especially their inflatable balls).

I suggested that to keep Kai busy, I would start training him for dock diving. It would give him a job and hopefully wear him out a bit so when he went home with the boys; he would be calm and relaxed. I even said I was going to enter Kai in a dock diving event, but I don't think my family thought I was serious. I found an event in upstate New York and entered it even though neither Kai nor I had ever attended one. We arrived at the event not really knowing what we were getting into, although I had read all the rules and tried to be as prepared as I could be (I sure didn't want to get embarrassed). We got to the event early to do two practice jumps before our scheduled jump. I don't know who was more nervous, Kai or me. I realized he was nervous when we had to walk up a flight of stairs onto the raised dock. I could see he was having trouble with all the smells he was dealing with coming from that dock, which had so many other dogs on it before him. This makes sense when you think about it: a dog's sense of smell, at minimum, is ten thousand times better than ours. His olfactory receptors must have been overwhelmed. This was different from jumping into our backyard pool at ground level with no other dogs around—not to mention the cheering audience.

From sled dogs to Dock Dogs: Kai loves the water
Photo credit: Bobby Kelly

I put him in his sit-stay position and walked to the end of the dock by the water. I released him, and he came charging down the dock at top speed. I threw the bumper, but as he got close to the end of the dock and realized how high we were in the air and how far down the water was, he put on the brakes and wouldn't jump. He stood there looking at me, like, *Really, you want me to jump from up here?* The event was at a county fair, and the grandstands were full. It was my worst nightmare! You could hear the groans from the crowd! *Now what?* I had one more practice jump. I knew Kai was obsessed with retrieving this bumper. Every time he came to our house, he would find it and bring it to me to throw for him. So, I decided on his second practice jump, I would run the dock beside him, rather than have him sit. I planned to get him all jacked up, keeping his bumper just away from him. When we both got to the end of the dock, instead of throwing the bumper, I planned to just drop it into the water to get him to jump off the end of the dock. I thought if I could get him in the water once, he would be good. He didn't need to jump far, just *jump*, and that is what he did! He basically just fell into the water to get the bumper. I felt we were over the hump: he was focused on the bumper, and now he had the confidence to jump. We were on our way.

On our first official jump, I didn't throw the bumper far; I just wanted Kai to jump in, and he did with no hesitation. I think his first jump was only four feet. After that, he was *all systems go*, flying and splashing down in the pool. Kai ended up winning the first event we ever attended! He went on to have a great first season, and he just loves it. My goal before we started was to see if he could jump fourteen feet. The sport is dominated by Labrador retrievers, Malinois, and Whippets, not Cattle Dogs. Kai now routinely jumps over eighteen feet. Our new goal is for Kai to qualify for the Dock Dogs World Championships. If we can accomplish that, I may be the first person ever to qualify for a world championship in sled dog racing and dock diving! Someone asked me what the difference is between training a sled dog and training a dock diving dog. I said about 80°F!

Kai bringing home the hardware in Dock Dogs, with me and Lucas,
my grandson who handles all of Kai's conditioning between events
Photo credit: Sarah Lowe

CHAPTER 24

❖

Tales from the Lecture Circuit

I have been fortunate enough to give lectures all around the world, and certainly, they don't always go as planned. One of the first of my lectures that went awry was in Turku, Finland, at the Sports and Exercise Medicine Research Center, where I was giving a lecture on feeding the canine athlete. I was invited to stay with a veterinarian who was also acting as my translator. Towards the end of the lecture, I started talking about the science behind replenishing muscle glycogen in running dogs post-exercise. I went on to say that dogs are not like people in that they don't need to replenish electrolytes like humans would by consuming something like Gatorade. (The reason is that dogs don't sweat—they may lose an insignificant amount through their pads, but not enough to need an electrolyte solution.) In fact, studies done years ago by the Army Quartermaster Corps have shown that giving electrolytes post-exercise to a dog can actually cause diarrhea and lead to dehydration, which you are trying to avoid. There were enough bilingual people in Finland who spoke very good English that she had to translate exactly what I said. I could tell this subject was not going over well with the entire audience. Suddenly, a group of people on one side of the auditorium started pointing and hollering at a group of people in another section of the room. I didn't know what was going on, but obviously, I said something that angered some of the crowd. It turned out that the veterinarian who was hosting me during the visit was selling an electrolyte solution to some retailers who were in attendance, and they, in turn, were selling it to the dog people in the audience, who were now very angry! This made for an uncomfortable couple of days. I couldn't wait to get back on the plane and return home. I am still very surprised how many doggy Gatorade products remain on the market. I think this goes back to the humanization of our pets, where pet parents think, *If it is good for me, it must be good for my dog.*

Another difficult situation occurred in Shanghai, China, at Pet Fair Asia, the biggest pet industry expo in the world. Event organizers assigned a young woman to act as my translator during my trip, which included a lecture on canine nutrition during the show. She was great all week. When I gave my talk, she and I stood up on stage at two podiums. I would say a couple of sentences in English, and then she would repeat them in Mandarin for the audience. I could see she was having trouble, and I realized I should have gone over some of the more scientific terms beforehand with her. But there really wasn't any time, as they kept me very busy and on a tight schedule. We weren't fifteen minutes into an hour-long lecture, and she completely cracked. I couldn't tell if she was laughing or crying, but she gave me this forlorn "I am sorry" look and ran off the stage! I stood there dumbfounded, frozen in time. *Now, what do I do?* I was just looking out into the audience for what seemed like forever. Thank goodness our Chinese distributor, Penny, came to the rescue. She is fluent in English and obviously Mandarin and had worked in the pet industry for many years, so she knew the terminology. She came up on stage and took her place at the translator's mic, and we went on to complete the lecture without missing a beat. Penny was a lifesaver!

Another lecture turned out to be quite entertaining and humorous, of course, at my expense. I was invited to speak to a group of sled dog people at an event put on in conjunction with Cornell University College of Veterinary Medicine. I had a couple of close friends who were on staff at the college, and they even offered to produce my slides for me (This was back before PowerPoint when lectures were given using slide projectors. Remember slides?). This was all the way back to the '90s when 35mm film negatives were projected on a screen. You had to have someone who could produce these slides—it was not as simple as making slides on your computer, as we all take for granted today. My friends at Cornell said they would have my slides produced there, which I thought was very nice of them. They even loaded them into the carousel for me, so all I had to do was show up and make my presentation. In fact, I never got a chance to look at the slides before my talk.

I was introduced as a companion animal nutritionist, president, CEO, and creator of Annamaet Petfoods. A deep dive into nutrition can honestly become kind of boring. Well, this turned out to be anything but boring. A handful of slides into my presentation, up popped a slide that said, "Studies have shown that dogs fed Annamaet dog food will gain 30 percent more weight than dogs fed nothing at all!" The audience went wild with laughter. I glared at my colleagues from Cornell, and they were all smirking, trying to look like they didn't have anything to do with it. I went on for a while, getting back on topic, and then up popped a slide that said, "Annamaet will put weight on a dead dog!" Of course, this was followed by another round of laughter. This went on for the entire lecture. They were all waiting for the next slide to embarrass me. Looking back, those slides certainly kept the audience's attention, and everyone enjoyed the lecture.

Not everyone pays attention to the speaker under the best of circumstances, especially when alcohol is involved. I was invited to be the after-dinner speaker at a Gun Dog of the Year awards ceremony sponsored by one of the big pet food companies. I thought it funny that they would invite me to speak, seeing as I own my own pet food company, but I guess they figured at the time we were so small that we weren't real competition. I knew some of the nutrition people at that company, and they trusted that with my background in training and feeding working dogs, I would give an entertaining presentation and be professional enough not to make it an Annamaet sales pitch. Before the presentation, I checked into my room provided by the sponsoring pet food company. *Wow!* This sure wasn't a room I was used to staying in when traveling on behalf of Annamaet. It was a multi-room suite with a canopy bed and double doors that opened to a large balcony.

I thought the talk went really well, and afterward, I was standing there congratulating myself, thinking, *Yep, you nailed it!* Then, the woman whose dog won the Gun Dog of the Year title came up to talk to me. She was from Alabama, as was the dog's trainer, and it was obvious she had been celebrating her win (she was inebriated). I loved that southern accent as she started to say, "I just want to tell you…" and I thought, *Here it comes, she is going to tell me what a great talk I gave!* But actually, she was saying, "I just want to tell you, you served a wonderful meal tonight; I really enjoyed it!" I was no longer feeling so high and mighty about the talk I gave. I did feel better a little later that night, back at the hotel bar, when the trainer of the winning gun dog kept asking me about training sled dogs.

He said, "You mean to tell me you can be running down the trail at twenty-plus miles per hour with ten dogs, and when you tell them to turn right or left, they just do it?" he asked me.

"Yes, sir!" I said.

"Damn, I thought I could train dogs!" he said. Then he asked again, "They turn just by hearing your command, no reins, e-collar, or anything?"

"It is all by voice."

"Damn, I thought I could train dogs!" he repeated.

I went off to bed thinking at least I made an impression on somebody!

◆

Until The Last Dog

eto's archenemy in the kennel was Reggae—a big, powerful dog that we acquired when he was a yearling along with his brother, Raven, who was an absolute sweetheart. Reggae would not take any foolishness from anybody; he was an alpha dog. Veto also thought he was king of the roost. Over the years, they had some battles—in fact, Veto had a pretty good scar on his face from one argument with Reggae. We were always trying to keep them apart, but when you have twenty-five dogs running free, that isn't always easy. When they reached about twelve years old, they decided to let bygones be bygones and became pretty good buddies. It was amazing to watch these old archenemies play together when they were out in the snow chasing a soccer ball or a Frisbee.

The day that Veto passed away was a particularly tough one for our family. After all those years raising and racing sled dogs, with often more than thirty-five dogs in the yard at one time, it never got any easier when a dog passed. This one might have been a little tougher than most, as Veto was very high energy and all personality—always wanting your attention and jealous of anybody who tried to get between you and him. In the dog barn, each dog has his own crate with a nice bed. Being creatures of habit, they always went to their own bed. We just opened the door, and they all ran in and jumped into their own crate. On the day of Veto's passing, when Mary Jo let the dogs back into the barn, Reggae ran into Veto's crate and laid on his bed. That night, after I let them out, he did the same thing. He just laid in Veto's bed. It really got to me.

Our kennel of dogs was basically one big pack: they always had each other—they were never by themselves. Mary Jo and I decided the last dog would move into the house so they wouldn't be alone out in the dog barn and kennel area. Of course, we could have no idea who the last dog would be. Over the years, a few dogs did transition into being good house dogs, but they weren't all happy to be inside. Salt was great in the house, although she always seemed to always be shedding.

I used to do talks at schools about education being the key to unlocking your future, describing how my own studies led me to sled dog racing and following my dreams. I would always bring a dog. One day, I decided to bring Espen with me, a big happy-go-lucky dog that I thought would be great with kids. The day before we went to school, I gave him a bath and decided to have him sleep in the house rather than run around in the kennel getting dirty. He really liked being in the house. We did the school talk, and Espen was great. He would spin around and rub his backside against a kid to have them rub his back end. Cats will often do that, but I have never seen a dog do it. When we got home, I opened the door and let Espen out, thinking he would run down to the dog barn. Instead, he ran to the front door of the house. Mary Jo let him in, and he never left!

The last two sled dogs were Raven and Reggae, both more than sixteen years old. When Raven passed, that left Reggae as the last sled dog, and moving him into the house didn't go well. First, he didn't want to come inside, and once there, he didn't like it. He panted and paced around. Then he tried to attack one of our four rescue cats, but luckily, Alex was right there and saved Chase. That was strike one. Strike two and three came when we saw that Reggae was way too interested in Lucas, our first-born grandson, who was barely a toddler at the time. Reggae's interest in Lucas was scary—he looked like he might hurt him. We decided that Reggae had no interest in being a house dog, though I felt bad having Reggae down in the barn at night by himself. I decided this was the time to start writing this book that I had promised my sister I'd write one day. I put an old wooden rocking chair next to his dog bed in the dog barn, and I sat in the rocker and started to write. Each night, I would go down to the barn to write, and Reggae would lay on the bed as I worked. I brought him a couple of treats, and occasionally I would bring myself a beer. Eventually, Reggae would go off to bed, and I would head up to the house. Sitting in the woods, writing with my dog at my side was inspiring. There was no internet, no phone, no worries. I had thoughts of Thoreau and Walden Pond dancing in my head.

For the next several months, I spent every evening in the barn with Reggae and continued to write. During the day, he would have the run of the place. Our cats quickly figured out his routine. By then, he was old, and they did not seem worried about him. Reggae's health started to deteriorate, and we knew it was a matter of time. He'd had a great life, but we all know Father Time is undefeated. One day, I was preparing to head to a pet industry trade fair, and Mary Jo and I were worried he might not be there when I got home. Before I left, I said goodbye to him, just in case. It was an emotional time.

This book started when all his brothers were gone. I didn't want our last sled dog to feel alone. I end this book by telling you that Reggae died peacefully during a rare March snowstorm. He was not alone; Mary Jo was by his side, cuddled up in the dog barn, which they all loved so much. It soon became apparent to us that the name of this book must be

Until The Last Dog.

Acknowledgments

◆

I want to thank my wife Mary Jo for keeping me grounded, focused and all her efforts in editing this book. I would like to thank my daughter Sarah, her husband Mike Lowe, my son Alex and his wife Madison Iversen for all the help and unwavering support they have provided. A special shout out to my grandsons Lucas, Jackson, Beckett and Finn for making me laugh and keeping me young.

I would like to thank my siblings and their spouses, who have always been there for me throughout my life. Pat and Dick Honkonen, Lou Ann and Jerry Greener, John and Cher Downey, my late sister and brother-in-law Fran and Art Skufca, my late brother Patrick and his widow Linda Downey, and Mary Beth and Keith Manninen. My mom, Anna Mae, my dad, Leo, who I remember telling me that the dog almost never makes a mistake, it is usually you as the handler and trainer who has screwed up. Thanks dad!

My lower 48 lifelong dog friends who were great training and traveling partners. Ted and Shirley Wallace, Alan and Annie Peters, Harris and Ginger Dunlap, Dr. Dawn Brown, Grahame and Sue Howe, Ralph Mitchell, Gary Callahan, Johnn and Nancy Molburg, Scott and Ginny Pirmann, Dr. Heather Huson, "The Flying Grandma" Joan Carlson, and Dr Joe Wakshlag. We could always count on Dr. Jeannie Ludlow to provide top veterinary care. My dear Alaskan friends who were always there for us - providing guidance, and a helping hand. Harvey Drake and Linda Leonard, Kathy Frost and her late husband Lloyd Lowry, Eric and Stacy Lanser, Charlie Champaine, Roxy Wright, Terri Killam, Dr. Arleigh Reynolds, and the best Race Marshall around, Mike McCowan. Always there to help control our crazy dogs in the starting chute were Edie Forrest and Andrea Swingley.

A big thank you to our dear Canadian friends who always provided a warm place to stay, a hot meal, and great training trails as we made our way across the Trans Canada and Alaska Highways on our way to Alaska. Terry and Debbie Streeper, Ross and Tammy Saunderson, and Don and Faye Cousins. We also couldn't have done it without long time corporate sponsors like Annamaet Petfoods, Risdon Rigs and the John Calvitti Company.

I must also thank one of my best friends, Kit Brown, who was with Annamaet Petfoods almost from the beginning until his untimely passing in 2022. He was a fearless veteran Marine who could always make me laugh. He also taught me to appreciate single malt scotch. He may be gone but he will never be forgotten.

Author Bio

Rob Downey's lifelong involvement with dogs has led to a career as a companion animal nutritionist. His research has been published in several peer reviewed Veterinary and Nutrition journals. His first book, *Until The Last Dog*, follows the path of his compelling life story, from early childhood trauma to competing in sled dog sports for close to 40 years, including twenty winters in Alaska. Rob has traveled the world giving lectures. He calls beautiful Bucks County Pennsylvania home where he lives with his lovely wife Mary Jo and their rescue animals, Lee, an Australian Cattle Dog and a very vocal orange tabby cat they call Chase.

17f63c48-b0fb-4df1-a00d-a5ffe29044ffR01